Adoption in Brief

Alan A. Jacka,

OBE, MA.

Research and Other Literature in the
United States, Canada and Great Britain,
1966-72: An Annotated Bibliography

 NFER

Published by the NFER Publishing Company Ltd

Registered Office: The Mere, Upton Park, Slough, Bucks, SL1 2DQ

Book Division: 2 Jennings Buildings, Thames Avenue,
Windsor, Berks, SL4 1QS

First Published 1973

© *National Children's Bureau 1973*

SBN 85633 015 9

Printed in Great Britain by
Direct Design (Bournemouth) Ltd., 12 Roumelia Lane, Boscombe,
Bournemouth, Hampshire

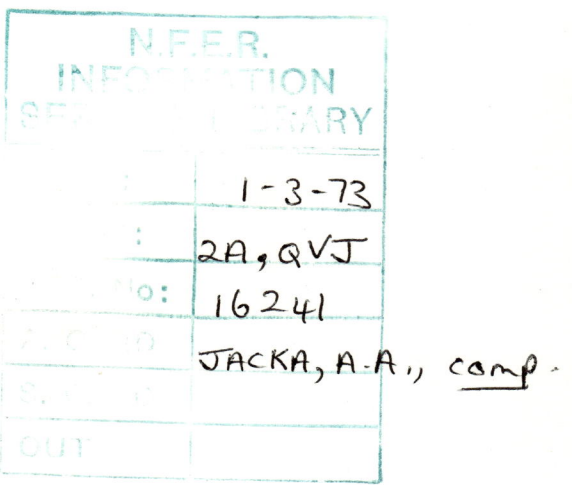

CONTENTS

FOREWORD

Over 200,000 children have been adopted in the last ten years. Over 400,000 people have adopted them, and at least half a million other people are close relatives of the adopters, and so personally interested in what has taken place.

It is to these people, as well as to those professionally concerned with adoption and to members of responsible committees in voluntary and statutory adoption agencies, that this brief summary of information is addressed.

Great interest was aroused by the findings of the Departmental Committee which reconsidered the whole matter of adoption. The field was covered effectively and thoroughly in 1966 in a 'Review of Research in the United States, Canada and Great Britain between 1948 and 1965' published under the title *Adoption — Facts and Fallacies* by M.L. Kellmer Pringle (Longman, in association with the National Children's Bureau).

This volume attempts to do two things. The first is to bring the list of research work up to date, and it covers some two hundred items — books, articles and research reports — published since 1965, with short abstracts or annotations and sufficient indication of the source to make reference to the full text easily possible. Some of the material is in British and American journals, some in unpublished theses, some in full-length books.

The research is reviewed in four sections, in each of which the entries are arranged by author in alphabetical order. They are numbered consecutively throughout, irrespective of sections. At the end of the book there is an index listing all authors alphabetically with dates of works in brackets and reference by entry number.

The second thing is to put the overall picture in a short form so as to be readily available to students, practitioners, committee members, and the large section of the general public interested in adoption for one reason or another.

The material in each part is arranged as far as possible in successive sections dealing with (a) the facts, (b) the questions and (c) the fallacies.

OVERVIEW

WHO SHOULD ADOPT?

(a) *What is known*

A great deal of the thinking and research about adoption has been concerned with the selection of the right couples with whom to place a child, and with follow-up studies to assess the results.

The most certain thing that is known about the adoption process is that its 'success' depends more than anything else on the adopting couple, and on their having the right attitude to children — and of course this is not very easy to define in precise and measurable terms. Nevertheless one can say that the weight of evidence shows the positive association of successful and happy adoptions judged over short periods and long periods with such things as:

a warm and accepting attitude on the part of the adopters to children;

a recognition and acceptance by the adopters of the adopting role;

a warm, stable adopting family;

a sensible and understanding attitude to infertility, illegitimacy, and the natural parents on the part of the adopting parents themselves and their relatives, particularly the grandparents.

(Bradley 1967, Lawder 1969, McWhinnie 1967, Seglow *et al* 1972).

These all seem to be more important in the long run than such things as:

the age of the adopting parents;

their education;

their socio-economic status; or

the kind of child they adopt.

(McWhinnie 1967, Kornitzer 1968, Seglow *et al.* 1972).

(b) *What is under consideration*

Among the points that have been recommended for official consideration and possible action, affecting the selection of adoptive parents, are:

5

the exclusion of parents, grandparents and other relatives from adoption, and the provision of a form of guardianship as an alternative (Association of C.C.O. 1969, Advisory Council 1970, Home Office 1970, 1972);
the exclusion of single persons.
There is some conflict of evidence about such things as the effect of:
the age of the adopting mother. Some find the older married couple better at coping with the older child, and some find that the younger mother is more successful (Kornitzer 1971, McWhinnie 1967);
the presence of other children in the family. Some found this linked with failure (Kadushin and Seidl 1970), and others found it a favourable influence (Jaffee and Fanshel 1970).

(c) *What is clearly not true*
Misleading assumptions about adoption are all too many, and among those that can usefully be listed are:
that a success rate can be reliably established;
that there is no difference between an adopted family and a natural family (Kadushin 1970, Sensel and Yeakel 1970);
that adopted children are not interested in, and do not need to talk about, their adoption and their 'real' parents because they do not ask.

WHICH CHILDREN?

(a) *What is known*
There has been a steady and cumulative movement, both in this country and in America, away from the search for 'nice' lovable children, who can be fitted into 'nice' homes, to the search for families that will provide the right sort of home for the children who *need* them, and of course this includes the 'hard-to-place' children with obvious need, but some characteristics that make them less than lovable at first sight: those who are no longer babies; those with some physical or mental limitation or handicap; those who are 'non-white'.
It may be claimed that this has happened because there has been a drying up of the supply of 'babies suitable for adoption'. But there is more to it than this. There is an accumulation of evidence that, on the one hand suitable families *can* be found for such children (Knight 1970, Fischer 1971); on the other hand, that the placements work out satisfactorily (Fischer 1971, Franklin and Massarik 1969); and finally, the adopting parents find satisfaction of the right sort (Franklin and Massarik 1969). That is to say that this is not a makeshift, second-class arrangement which the adopters put up with *faute de mieux*.
This does not mean that every child in care should be adopted out of hand. The consent of the natural parent(s) is essential. Some children do *not* in fact

respond well to a placement, but fewer than was once supposed, and many of these can in fact tolerate a second placement and find happiness in it (Kadushin and Seidl 1970).

Historically this all seems to stem from the work of Skeels and others who were able to show conclusively that children of low-calibre parents (judged by intellectual, educational and socio-economic standards) when placed in suitable adoption homes, eventually developed so well that they were up to or above the average population in ability and adjustment, and maintained their level over the years (Skeels 1965).

This does not mean of course that it does not matter what the background of a child is, at what age he is placed for adoption, how many 'homes' he has previously known, and what his physical and mental endowment is. It does mean that the kind of home he eventually finds himself in, and the attitude of the adopting parents and their relatives, are of over-riding importance, and are in the long run decisive (Kadushin 1970, Kadushin and Seidl 1970, Seglow, Kellmer Pringle and Wedge 1972). In the right home children seem to be able very largely to overcome their initial handicaps.

(b) *What is under consideration*
The exploration of the question 'Which children?' has led to such a broadening of the definition of 'adoptable', that there is just the danger that one may end up with the proposition 'Any child is adoptable . . .' which inevitably finishes with the qualification '. . . if the right adopters can be found'.

And in fact the limits have been found to be very wide. It is no longer necessary to exclude the baby with poor genetic endowment, nor the mentally or physically handicapped. But it is also agreed (Knight 1970) that it would be unwise to go so far as to include in this broad category the severely subnormal or the grossly handicapped.

What is 'severe' and what is 'gross' in this context? This we must continue to explore and clarify by particular examples — though there will of course always be a twilight area of uncertainty.

There are several matters which require much more precise knowledge to enable adopters and supporting social workers to help adopted children with some of their needs. The age and method of telling children what they need to know about themselves so as to achieve a clear sense of identity based on fact not fantasy — these are matters on which the theoretical general truth is clear, but the details imprecise (Lawder 1970, McWhinnie 1967). Several of these questions have been submitted to the Houghton Committee and they are referred to below in the administrative and legal section, for they concern the happiness and rights of the adopted children themselves very closely.

Perhaps the outstanding question is how to help the children (admittedly a very small number), whose adoption is refused by a court, and the very much larger number (very considerable indeed one suspects) who are never placed for adoption because the necessary consent is not forthcoming when they are babies, and who then fall into the 'hard-to-place' or 'unadoptable' class. And those many others, who through mental, physical or social handicap (including racial reasons) are at present never even considered for placement (Chambers 1970).

(c) *What is clearly not true*
Perhaps the biggest fallacy is to suppose that *any* child is unadoptable, unless his physical or mental handicap is so gross that even if he were the biological child of a family, that family could not care for him without impairing or destroying its own continued existence. Somewhere there may well be a couple who could and would undertake the extra responsibility of most 'hard-to-place' children, and find satisfaction in doing so, and to judge by the information available, a degree of success that makes it well worth taking trouble about.

Though there are good theoretical reasons why one might expect children offered for adoption to be at a greater risk of developing personality problems such as emotional maladjustment and delinquency, (as a result, for example, of the disturbing effects of illegitimate birth; the stress in which his infancy is likely to have passed; the effect of social disapproval of the illegitimate child, even though less now than it once was; the effect of being one of a minority class — the 'adopted'), there is also some evidence to show that these fears are not realized (Hoopes 1970, Elonen 1969, Seglow, Kellmer Pringle and Wedge 1972).

WHOSE CHILDREN?

(a) *What is known*
The most striking facts about the people whose children have been adopted in this country in the recent past are threefold, and they are inter-related. They are:
illegitimacy is no longer a class phenomenon, since the mothers of illegitimate children are found in all the socio-economic classes in the same proportion as the mothers of legitimate children (Crellin, Kellmer Pringle and Wedge 1972);
there is a changed and much less censorious attitude to unmarried mothers and illegitimacy in society as a whole; and finally
a dwindling number of babies are being offered for adoption (Carriline 1970).

The first of these is a simple statistical fact.

The second has led to much more determined

efforts being made by the professional social workers concerned to give the mother of an illegitimate child the chance to keep her child. Mother and baby homes have been closing all over the country, and flatlets for the mothers to make a home for themselves and their children have been established in a number of places. Organisations as widely different as the National Council for the Unmarried Mother and Her Child, and Mothers in Action, represent this movement of public opinion, and social policy.

No doubt the number of babies offered for adoption has been, or will eventually be, affected by the availability of 'the pill' and the working of the Abortion Act, which have already stemmed the rising tide of illegitimate births† (Child Welfare 1970). The actual number has fallen slightly in England and Wales since 1967, and the percentage fell for the first time in 1968.

Only gradually is reliable evidence becoming available to show whether the greater stability of adoptive homes, and the more stimulating conditions in adoptive families, outweigh the advantages of a mother looking after her own baby. But what evidence there is points in that direction. (Crellin, Kellmer Pringle and West 1972).

(b) *What is under consideration*
Increasingly, however, attention is being directed, not solely to the resolution of the crisis produced by the birth of an illegitimate baby and plans for his care and nurture, but to a long-term plan for all concerned. This means a casework service, and any other services that are needed, for both of the natural parents, for adoptive and foster parents, and for any relatives who may be involved in plans for the child's long-term care. This service should be available before and after the birth of the child, and would be necessary whether the child is placed for adoption, or in a foster home, or in some other form of residential care (Home Office 1970, 1972).

This sort of pattern not only recognises the paramount importance of the welfare of the child, since he is growing up into a citizen who will be either a

†Registrar General's Statistical Review

	1960	1965	1966	1967	1968	1969	1970
Number of illegitimate live births	42,707	66,249	67,056	69,298	69,806	67,041	64,744
Percentage of all live births	5·4%	7·7%	7·9%	8·4%	8·5%	8·4%	8·3%

social asset or an expensive burden for many years to come, but it takes the same positive view of the natural mother, and also of the natural father — so long neglected in any thinking and provision hitherto made. These parents are citizens too, and like their child may be social assets or social risks (Burgess 1968, Home Office 1970, 1972).

The rapid growth of a network of children's departments throughout the country, and their reorganisation into social service departments, has meant that there has been a good deal of thinking and experience available about the structure of social service provision — the sort of thing that is needed and what it can do (Advisory Council 1970, Association of C.C.O. 1969, Gebbett 1971).

Increasingly it is being felt that the present arrangements for parental consent to the adoption of a child are fair neither to child, the adopters or the natural mother herself, since the consent is not final until the adoption order is actually made. The possibility of an irrevocable decision at some earlier date would remove the uncertainty and strain in the adoption home, and would relieve the natural mother of the impossible anxiety of knowing that she can change her mind again if she feels like it. She, of all people, needs help in making a decision and sticking to it, rather than being encouraged in her uncertainty over what is inevitably an agonising decision for her to have to make (Association of C.C.O. 1969, Festinger 1971, Home Office 1970, 1972).

ADMINISTRATIVE AND LEGAL MATTERS

Half a century after the first Adoption Act, a Departmental Committee was set up, and canvassed interested opinion by means of a Working Paper (Home Office 1970), in preparation for new legislation to bring the law and administration up to date.

(a) *What are the matters on which there is a high degree of unanimity?*
(Advisory Council 1970, Association of C.C.O. 1969).

Some can be listed without hesitation, as having a respectable history in the adoption literature, and as commanding the assent of official circles, the profession and the committee of enquiry (as suggested by its tentative 'propositions'):
the *welfare of the child* should be paramount, and stated to be so for legal purposes;
there should be some kind of *unified jurisdiction*, so that adoption applications would be heard in a suitable court that is concerned about other family matters, some of them contingent on the outcome of the adoption application. For instance:
the future welfare of a child should be safeguarded, when an application for his adoption has been *refused* by the court;
the *fathers* of children who are adopted should be

brought into the process more than at present, their rights should be more clearly defined, and a service provided to meet their own personal needs;
some form of *guardianship* should be made available to obviate the need for the subterfuge of adoption of children by their relatives.

(b) *Other matters which have less than unanimous support, but which are clearly due for review are:*
adoption agencies (whether voluntary or statutory) should be subject to the same, revised, regulations and the same central (not local authority) inspection and registration (Association of C.C.O. 1969);
some way should be found (perhaps by making the parental consent irrevocable at a reasonably early stage) of encouraging *early placement* of children, without the danger of 'snatch-backs' (Triseliotis 1969).

(c) *Finally, there is a whole list of matters which are strongly advocated in reputable quarters and on which there is sometimes a certain amount of research evidence, but which are still to some extent controversial:*
the importance of an adoption agency having the *full range of social services* (or at least children's services) at its disposal, and not being merely a placing agency (Association of C.C.O. 1969);
the importance of a *casework service* being readily available to all parties — natural mother and father, and adopting parents — before, during and after placement (Home Office 1970, 1972, Lawder 1970);
and the value of *group methods* — not least for the unsuccessful applicants for a child to adopt (Leeding 1970, Parfit 1972, Rowe 1966, Biskind 1966);
the desirability of adopted children having the right, at a suitable age, to have access to the *adoption records* (Home Office 1970, 1972, McWhinnie 1970);
a concerted attempt to place a greater proportion of hard-to-place children, at as early an age as possible by means such as:
the use of the *Adoption Resources* Exchange (Carriline 1970, Raynor 1971)
an educational and *publicity campaign*, continued over a period.
legalising payments in special cases, to enable a couple to adopt, for example, a number of children from one family together (Andrews 1968, Gentile 1970, Triseliotis 1970, Watson 1972).
One matter on which there is a sharp difference of opinion and on which the available evidence is not conclusive, is:
whether *direct and third part adoptions* are so risky that they should be forbidden, or whether overall they turn out much the same in the long run as the

most carefully 'matched' adoptions (Association of C.C.O. 1969, and Kornitzer 1968, Seglow *et al.* 1972).

PURPOSES AND
PRINCIPLES

(a) *Near certainties* or *Generally accepted*
Three purposes may be distinguished in the practice of adoption over the years:
finding a *home for a child;*
finding a *child for a home;*
building *a family.*

The kind of *de facto* adoption that was practised in England and Wales before adoption was legalized by the first Adoption Act in 1926 was quite simply finding 'a home for a child' who needed one, for only a limited number of couples were prepared to resort to this expedient to remedy childlessness.

Although the number of legalized adoptions built up gradually between the wars, it was not until after the Second World War that adoption became 'popular' and the number of applicants for children to adopt became so great that it was impossible to meet all demands. Circumstances therefore made the work of adoption agencies a matter of finding 'a child for a home'. Some agencies found themselves having to decide whether a 'fair distribution' meant that they should restrict the number of children placed in a family to one apiece, since there were so many childless couples clamouring for their 'fair share'. They also had to make the difficult choice between one family and another for the only baby available. Someone had to be refused; in fact more had to be refused than could be accommodated. The agencies found themselves using rule of thumb methods for selecting the homes where the limited number of available children should be placed. All sorts of ways of trying to suit the child to the home, and the home to the child were resorted to, so as to ensure the greatest likelihood of 'success'.

Of recent years there has been a further change in the attitude of placing agencies, who had meanwhile become much more professional in their outlook. They were more aware of the social consequences of the adoption process, and much more concerned with the long-term outcome of what they were doing in terms of the well-being of society — i.e. the importance of building a family, which might well mean adoptive families with one, two or more children, rather than a uniform range of 'only' children.

Recent studies of the practice of adoption agencies (Rose 1970, Triseliotis 1970) show that these purposes and principles have not always been clearly understood or formulated by those responsible, but that practice has followed the urgent needs and requirements of day to day problems.

Thinking has been stimulated and helped by the existence and work of organisations such as the

Association of British Adoption Agencies in this country, and the Child Welfare Bureau in America, which have brought together all concerned, both voluntary and statutory, and promoted discussion of both current practice and underlying principles.

One fundamental principle is generally agreed — that the welfare of the individual child should be considered paramount. On the one hand, it is held desirable (Triseliotis 1970) that this concept should be clarified; and on the other hand (Advisory Council 1970, A.C.C.O. 1969, Seglow *et al.* 1972) it is considered urgent that as a principle it should be enshrined in the law.

(b) *Matters under consideration*
Other matters which are also listed for early attention are:
a review of the function of case committees; and
a review of the financial aspects of adoption.

The case committee is one of the requirements of English law. But in some agencies, the respective functions of the members of the committee and the professional caseworkers are blurred. A worthwhile case committee should not be a 'rubber stamp' for decisions already taken; but neither should it assume the functions of a professional caseworker, when its members have neither the time, training or experience that is needed.

The financial provisions of adoption law stem from the purpose of the early legislation to make 'baby farming' illegal, if not impossible, and as a consequence the exchange of money is strictly controlled or forbidden. The situation is different today, and it seems as if an unnecessary financial burden is placed on eligible prospective adopters: to pay for medical examinations, to forego foster home payments, and to receive no payment or reimbursement of expenses in respect of the child placed with them. In the case of a couple, perhaps with children of their own already, who are prepared to accept two, three or even four brothers and sisters for adoption, the financial burden is sizeable, and limits the possibilities very much. Subsidized adoption in special cases of this sort is being explored in some states in America, since it makes adoption a possibility for children who otherwise would not be considered, without breaking up a united family of children.

Two points of principle which are of importance, but on which there are divergent views, passionately held, are:
that there should be maximum free communication between all parties — adopters, agency, child, natural parents, and the public; and
that legal adoption should not be used as a subterfuge to conceal illegitimacy, by relatives adopting a son, a grandson or a nephew (Association of C.C.O. 1969).

The elements of secrecy and anonymity in the adoption process are understandable, but on the whole make for uncertainty, anxiety and difficulty. Much of the difficulty experienced by adopting families stems from some lack of communication; the child not being told the facts about himself; the adopting parents being worried about natural parents they know little about; rejected applicants wondering what is wrong with them; bereft mothers wondering whether they have done the right thing; and the public treating adopted children as peculiar because they know too little about the whole matter, and imagine there are skeletons in cupboards that are really empty.

If the welfare of the child should be paramount, then he should not suffer any stigma from his illegitimacy. But to use legal adoption to cover it up, by pretending that his grandmother or his aunt is his mother, is a wrong use of the legal process and confusing to the child in his search for his proper identity. So runs the argument, and as we have seen above, a number of authorities are anxious that some form of guardianship should be explored for some of these circumstances (Association of C.C.O. 1969, Home Office 1970, 1972).

POSTSCRIPT

In general social terms, adoption is one of the soundest, most lasting — and incidentally cheapest — ways of meeting the needs of certain children, who are socially deprived and in need of a normal home life. The risks attached to failure are not inconsiderable, but the proportion of satisfactory placements is high.

It is all the more important therefore that the law, the administrative arrangements, and the practice of the adoption agencies should be geared to achieving their purpose, and that this purpose should be the right one. It is hoped that the synopsis of the main elements in the discussion, given in the previous pages, will enable this purpose to be more clearly defined; and so for those concerned to see that any legislative changes make for the welfare of the children, the proper protection of parental and family rights, and the satisfaction of those undertaking the upbringing of children by adopting them. These are the results that it is to be hoped may flow from legislation based on the recent 'Report of the Departmental Committee on the Adoption of Children' (Home Office and Scottish Education Department, 1972).

ANNOTATED BIBLIOGRAPHY

SECTION I   Research

1 ADAMS, MORTON, S., DAVIDSON, RUTH, T. and CONNELL, PHYLLIS (1967)	'Adoptive risks of the children of incest — a pre-liminary report'. *Child Welfare*, vol. 46, no. 3, pp. 137—42. Report of a study undertaken by the Department of Human Genetics at the University of Michigan, comparing 18 cases of incest and 18 matched controls. Elements characteristic of brother/sister and father/daughter matings are enumerated and discussed. Early identification of cases of incest is important, and also measures to identify congenital abnormality. Larger samples are needed for final evaluation of the effects of incest.
2 ADRIAN, R.J., VACCHIANO, R.B. and GILBART, T.E. (1966)	'Linear discriminant function classification of accepted and rejected adoptive parents', *Journal of Clinical Psychology*, vol. 22, no. 2, pp. 251—54. A careful exploration of the use of objective psychological tests as part of the basis for selecting adoptive parents. The results were so little in agreement with the independent judgements of adoption agencies, that it was concluded the tests have little practical utility in classifying adoptive applicants.
3 BOHMAN, MICHAEL (1970)	*Adopted children and their families*. A follow-up study of adopted children, their background, environment and adjustment. Proprius, Stockholm, 240 pp. This is a follow-up of a representative group of adopted children and their families, undertaken some ten years after the children were placed through the Adoption Agency of the Child Welfare Committee of Stockholm City. The sample was the 168 children (93 boys and 75 girls) placed by the agency within a period of two years. Ages ranged from ten to eleven

years. The adoptive parents were found to have a better attitude towards girls than boys, and the girls were better adjusted, both in the home and at school. Maladjustment was more frequently found among boys than girls. Problem behaviour was characterized by disturbed relations with peers, defiance, aggressiveness and inability to concentrate.

4 BRADLEY, TRUDY (1966)

'An exploration of caseworkers' perceptions of adoptive applications', *Child Welfare*, vol. 45, no. 8, pp. 433—43.
See below — BRADLEY 1967.

5 BRADLEY, TRUDY (1967)

An exploration of caseworkers' perceptions of adoptive applicants. Final report project no. R-4, U.S. Children's Bureau, New York, Child Welfare League of America, xi, 225 pp.
A study of the assessment and selection procedures in eight adoption agencies in one state in U.S.A. Among the more interesting conclusions are:
the smaller proportion of Negro couples who were accepted, and the larger proportion of accepted Negro couples who withdrew;
the apparent advantage of couples who had already adopted, and the disadvantage of those who already had children of their own;
the desirability of devoting more time to rejected applicants;
the need for scrutiny of the qualifications of adoption caseworkers, with possible suggestions for schools of social work.
In addition there are considerations arising from:
the age of children at placement; and
the smaller number of placements of Negro children and of children of mixed racial origin.
From the scrutiny of caseworkers' assessments there emerged:
the importance of three factors: positive psychosocial appraisal, suitability of a home for a deviant child, and young marriage;
some reflections on the matching of 'better' and 'marginal' children with 'better' and 'marginal' homes.

6 BRATFOS, O., EITINGER, L. and TAU, T. (1968)

'Mental illness and crime in adopted children and adoptive parents', *Acta psychiatr. scand. Danem.*, 44, no. 4, pp. 376—84, bibl.
This study covers 250 children adopted before the age of seven in Norway during the period 1935—1939 by non-relatives, and the 243 adoptive mothers and 239 adoptive fathers concerned. The results showed a total of 19 adopted children, and 38 adoptive parents, who appeared in the official files in the following categories: oligophrenia, psychoses, neuroses and other disorders, alcoholism, crime. The results do not indicate that adopted children differ in any special way from the rest of the population, nor that

these problems in adopted children could be traced back to the adoptive parents.

7 CRELLIN, EILEEN,
KELLMER PRINGLE,
M.L. and WEST,
PATRICK (1971)

Born Illegitimate. Social and Educational Implications. National Foundation for Educational Research, 173 pp.

This study provides descriptive material about a national sample of 679 children born in 1958, compares their development with that of other children born in the same week, and relates their development at the age of seven years to a range of factors linked with their birth history as well as with their mothers' social and personal background. Most of the factors presented statistically are arranged under the headings legitimate, illegitimate and pre-marital conception, or where appropriate, legitimate, illegitimate and adopted.

One unexpected finding was that there was no difference in social background and upbringing between mothers having respectively a legitimate or illegitimate baby. On every count children born illegitimately were found to be at an initial disadvantage, and this disadvantage persisted throughout the first seven years, except for those children who were adopted. The favourable environment of the adopted children was found to halt or even reverse the effects of early disadvantages or deprivations.

The implications for social policy are worked out under the heads of primary, secondary and tertiary prevention; and a strong plea is made for the long-term welfare of the child being the first and paramount consideration.

8 CUNNINGHAM,
JAMES, J. (1969)

'A comparison of adopted and non-adopted emotionally disturbed adolescents and their parents', in *Dissertation Abstracts International*, vol. 30 (1-B), pp. 378—9.

This study of the relationship between adoption and child-rearing attitudes (Authoritarian Control and Parental Warmth) is based on results obtained from eighty emotionally disturbed adolescents (40 adopted and 40 non-adopted). Results did not support the expectation of a significant difference between adoptive and non-adoptive families' attitudes regarding authoritarian control, nor a greater level of agreement regarding child rearing attitudes among non-adopted children and their parents than among adopted children and their parents, nor that the child rearing attitudes of the adoptive families would be more punitive.

9 DINNAGE,
ROSEMARY (1967)

'Research on adoption', *Case Conference*, vol. 13, no. 10, pp. 357—60.

A critical review article about 'Adoption — Facts and Fallacies' (Kellmer Pringle 1967), picking out some of the topics not yet conclusively covered by research findings.

10 ELONEN, ANNA and
SCWARTZ, EDWARD M.
(1969)

'A longitudinal study of emotional, social and academic functioning of adopted children, *Child Welfare*, vol. 48, no. 2, pp. 72—8.

A follow-up study was made of 43 children placed by Chicago agencies, who were tested before placement and again after the age of sixteen. The only way in which the adopted children suffered by comparison with the non-adopted was in educational difficulties. Otherwise it seemed that the difficulties of both adopted and non-adopted children stemmed from their parents' reactions to them, to their questions and feelings, and to important events in family life.

11 FALK, L.L. (1970)

'Comparative study of transracial and inracial adoptions', *Child Welfare*, vol. 49, no. 2, pp. 82—8.

Conclusions are drawn about the families who undertake transracial adoption and inracial adoption based on questionnaires answered by matched couples in ten Midwestern states.

12 FESTINGER,
TRUDY BRADLEY
(1971)

'Unwed mothers and their decisions to keep or surrender children', *Child Welfare*, vol. 50, no. 4, pp. 253—61.

Variables consistently associated in this study and others with mothers' decisions to keep their children are listed: older age, employment status (not in school) and non-intact parental home. Some others add lower education. The decision to keep a child may be the result of a host of emotional needs and conflicts. The consistent finding that women who come from broken homes are more likely to keep their children may be related.

13 FRANKLIN, D.S. and
MASSARIK, F. (1969)

'Adoption of children with medical conditions', condensed version of report by the Children's Home Society of California, Los Angeles, in *Child Welfare*, vol. 48, no. 8, pp. 459—67, no. 9, pp. 533—9, no. 10, pp. 595—601.

From 449 placements over a ten-year period, a sample of 169 cases were studied, with a control group of 70. It was found that the more important factor in the outcome of the adoption was not the medical condition of the child but the delay in placing him, while medical tests were carried out; and that the medical condition did not significantly interfere with the satisfaction found by the parents, i.e. in the 'adoptability' of the child. Two types of successful adopters emerged. One in the less well educated, blue-collar, craftsman class; the other in the affluent, well-educated class; both however were alike in being more interested in the child's worth than in his ability to realize their own expectations for him; they took a hopeful encouraging attitude while accepting his slow rate of progress. Some deductions about the agency's methods in such cases were made.

14 GOCHROS,
HARVEY L. (1967)

'A study of the caseworker-adoptive parent relationship in post-placement services', *Child Welfare*, vol. 46, no. 6, pp. 317—25, 348.

The main points emerging from this study are that there is no concensus on the role of the post-placement caseworker — probation or help-giving — and that to be effective the post-placement visits should be frequent and more closely spaced.

15 HARTLEY, RUTH E. (1969)

'Children's perceptions of sex preference in four culture groups', *Journal of Marriage and the Family*, vol. 31, no. 2, pp. 380—7.

Four hundred and eight children of five and eight years old, of four different culture groups, were separately interviewed, — Caucasian (Honolulu), European (New Zealand), Maori (New Zealand) and Americans of Japanese origin (Honolulu). They were shown pictures, and told an adoption story. Their reactions were noted on the choice of a boy or girl by the adopters to determine whether they noticed 'culturally determined male sex preference', and whether there was any difference accounted for by their cultural background. It appeared that at this age young children were not affected in their perceptions by their cultural background, and that they did not in general distinguish a 'culturally determined male sex preference', indeed in three of the four culture groups there was a trend towards recording a preference for females.

16 HERZOG, E., SUDIA, CECELIA, E. and HARWOOD, JANE

'Some opinions on finding families for black children', *Children*, vol. 18, no. 4, pp. 143—8.

A summary of the main findings of a study of the opinions of 100 experienced people in five cities reported in *Families for Black Children*, Herzog *et al.* (U.S. Government Printing Office) and includes the reasons given why people don't adopt, including agency-centred deterrents, and the possibility of placing children with single adopters, families of another race, older people, or those who need some financial subsidy. Methods of recruitment are also discussed.

17 HOOPES, JANET L. *et al.* (1970)

A follow-up study of adoptions. Vol. II. *Post-placement functioning of adopted children.* Child Welfare League of America. 126 pp.

The study makes an assessment of the functioning of a random sample of adopted children, compared with a sample of non-adopted children. With the exception of significantly fewer adopted children being rated 'excellent' by their teachers for adjustment and achievement, there was little difference between the two groups, and no evidence that the adopted children showed greater emotional problems or psychopathology.

The child's functioning did not appear to be affected by the age of the adoptive parents; but there was a positive link between the ability of the adoptive father to discuss infertility, and the outcome of the adoption.

18 HUMPHREY, MICHAEL (1969)

The Hostage Seekers — A Study of Childless and Adopting Couples. Longmans, in association with the National Children's Bureau, 162 pp.

A study of 80 childless couples, all of whom had attended an infertility clinic during a ten-year period, half had adopted, half were childless, and the aim was to explore the mental health aspects of infertility and adoption. The infertile husband was more likely to find himself an adoptive father, whereas the infertile wife was more likely to remain childless. Where both husband and wife regarded their parents as happily married, adoption was most likely to be acceptable. The advice of adoption workers about telling the child about his origins had been inadequate and at times downright inept. Some of the childless couples had achieved a deeply satisfying relationship, and there was no evidence that childlessness impaired sexual adjustment. Adopting couples could usefully have been given more detailed knowledge of the natural parents. Finally a marriage without children may be restricting rather than liberating to the marriage partners.

19 ILLINGWORTH, R.S. (1969)

'Assessment for adoption. A follow-up study', *Acta Paediatr. Scand.*, 58, no. 1, pp. 33—6.

A follow-up at school age of children who had been assessed in early infancy, most of them before twelve months. It showed a tendency to underestimate ability in infancy. It also showed the school age rating of 21 children of mentally defective parents averaged 100·1, 12 of them over 110, and one 125.

20 JACKSON, LYDIA (1968)

'Unsuccessful adoptions; a study of 40 cases', *British Journal of Medical Psychology*, vol. 41, part 4, pp. 389—98.

A careful study of 40 cases of adopted children referred to a child guidance clinic, from which it appeared that success cannot be assured by arranging the adoption at an early age, or telling the child about his adoption in good time. There is evidence to show that a decisive factor was incompatibility between child and adopters, particularly the adoptive mother, and elements of neurosis or character disorder in her. Statistics are methodically presented and six cases are described to show the characteristic features of the children's condition.

21 JAFFEE, BENSON and FANSHEL, DAVID (1970)

How they fared in adoption; a follow-up study. Columbia University Press, 370 pp.

The outcome of some 100 adoptions made by four

agencies were studied some 20 to 30 years after placement, by means of interviewing the adoptive parents. The views of the adopted children themselves, adults by now, were not taken into consideration. 'Forty per cent of the families interviewed indicated that they saw no major limitations in the adoptee with respect to his current functioning'. Other major findings were that boys fared somewhat less well than girls; that the number of pre-adoption placements did not significantly affect the eventual outcome; that there was no relationship between the adopted child's adjustment and the arrival of other, natural or adopted, children in the family subsequent to his adoption, while the presence of other children prior to it seemed to exert a favourable influence on adjustment and attainment. The authors 'were impressed by their failure to establish the expected relationship between the age of the adoptees at the time they were placed and their subsequent adjustment'. And rather surprisingly 'children who grew up in higher status families tended to encounter more personality problems than did their counterparts in lower status families'.

22 KADUSHIN, ALFRED (1967)

'Reversibility of trauma: a follow-up study of children adopted when older', *Social Work*, vol. 12, no. 4, pp. 22—33.

Ninety-one children who had been adopted when five years of age or older, and who had been removed from home by court order because of neglect or cruelty or both, were followed up in adolescence. In spite of their disturbed emotional history in infancy, and the fact that they had experienced on average two to three changes of home before adoptive placement, 80 to 82 per cent of the adoptions were assessed to be successful. This means that the effects of the early experiences were not in general irreversible. In a discussion of the results, an attempt is made to identify the factors associated with success, and other studies are quoted.

23 KADUSHIN, ALFRED (1970)

Adopting Older Children, Columbia University Press, 245 pp.

A study of 91 children (49 boys and 42 girls) of ages ranging from five to eleven years whose parents had been deprived of parental rights on account of neglect or ill-treatment of the children, and who were subsequently adopted between 1952 and 1962. All children were white and mentally and physically normal. All had been placed by one agency in Wisconsin, and the follow-up took place on average six years after placement. Compared with other adoption studies, the success rate is similar (74 per cent successful, 15 per cent unsuccessful and 11 per cent equivocal), in spite of the very bad early upbringing of the children in Kadushin's study. He concludes that there has been a tendency 'to over-emphasise the importance, significance and power of the past. . . . Agencies can take risks in placing older children with a high probability of success'.

24 KADUSHIN, ALFRED and SEIDL, FREDERICK, W. (1970)

Adoption Failure — A social work post-mortem. (Unpublished), 62 pp. (typescript).

A follow-up study of adoptions during the year immediately following placement, using as the criterion of failure the return of the child to the agency at any time for any reason, following placement and before legal adoption. The failure rate was 2·8 per cent for the 2,845 children placed in the years 1960--7 by the Wisconsin State Department of Health and Social Services. This compares with overall failure rate of adoption agency placements of about 1·7 per cent. The elements linked with failure seemed to be: children placed when they were two years of age or older; multiple sibling placements; adoptive families with adopted or 'own' children already in the home; adoptive parents who were older and had been married longer. About 50 per cent of the 'failures' were subsequently placed successfully for adoption. It is suggested that 'interlocutory decrees at the time of placement be given active consideration, and the time between placement and legal adoption be reduced'.

25 KIRK, D., JONASSOHN, K., FISH, A. (1966)

'Are adopted children especially vulnerable to stress?' *Archives of General Psychiatry*, vol. 14, pp. 291—8.

A statistical study of the use of five different clinics and clinic groups to discover if there were any above average proportion of adopted children. The results are inconclusive, though they challenge the conclusions of Schechter, *Arch.Gen.Psychiatry*, vol. 3, 1960, and Toussieng, *Child Welfare*, vol. 41, 1962. The difficulty is to get a random sample for study, and this (and a reliable figure for the proportion of adopted children in the American population) proves difficult.

26 KORNITZER, MARGARET and ROWE, JANE (1968)

Some casework implications in the study of children reclaimed or returned before final adoption. Standing Conference of Societies Registered for Adoption, 10 pp.

A study was made of the 161 children reclaimed by their natural mothers after placement for adoption, and the 96 children returned to the societies after placement. These represented respectively 2·1 per cent and 1·1 per cent of the 7,824 children placed by the 44 societies. The results are discussed.

27 LAWDER, ELIZABETH A. (1969)

A follow-up study of adoptions: post-placement functioning of adoption families. Child Welfare League of America, 232 pp.

A sophisticated study of 200 white families who

had adopted 250 children through the Children's Aid Society of Pennsylvania from three to ten years previously. Both postal questionnaires and intensive interviewing were used. The factors associated with success are presented in a variety of ways, correlated and cross-correlated, and representative samples of family life adjustments are described. The family factors most important in these ratings are:
satisfaction in parental role;
acceptance of adoptive role; and
warmth and affection towards the child.
and the child variables most closely related to out-come were:
development of conscience in the child;
social development of the child; and
child's need for outside help — as seen by the parents.
In addition, further examination of the data showed that adverse situations in the child's background and in the family situation may be successfully worked through, and a number of seemingly inappropriate placements in fact worked out well.

The case histories suggest ways of reducing the inevitable risk in adoption, and draw attention to the importance of the 'matching' process and of the case-work service provided by the adoption agency before, during, and after adoption.

28 LAWDER, ELIZABETH A. (1970)

'Post-adoption counselling: a professional obligation', *Child Welfare*, vol. 149, no. 8, pp. 435—42.

A study of 71 post-adoption counselling cases occurring in a five-year period in the Children's Aid Society of Pennsylvania. Of these families, 17 were black, and of the 109 children concerned, 22 were black. It was found that the interrelated factors of family expectations and the child's ability to establish healthy feelings of identity were linked with the outcome of adoption; and secondly that the most powerful therapeutic elements in these counselling cases were the agency as the symbol of continuity to the child, and as symbolic parent to the adoptive family.

29 McWHINNIE, ALEXINA M. (1967)

Adopted children; how they grow up; a study of their adjustment as adults. Routledge & Kegan Paul, 302 pp.

A book based on research into the individual case histories of 58 adults, 52 of whom had been adopted in childhood, and six of whom had been in long-term foster homes. Among the conclusions and recom-mendations are:
it was an advantage for the adoptive mother to be under 40;
factors other than high material standards and good educational standards are essential;
rigid religious views are a danger;
the age of the child at the time of adoption becomes a significant feature after two years old;

more important than family pattern (only child, other children and their ages, etc.) were basic attitudes of parents to all the children such as: a stable family life, both parents offering emotional security, acceptance, consistent discipline, encouragement and freedom;
right attitude to natural parents and illegitimacy;
absence of demand for gratitude;
importance of the attitude of the whole family;
the importance of the child being told about his adoption before the age of five years old;
recommended that access to factual information about natural parents should be made available to adopted children at a suitable age;
the duties of the guardian *ad litem* should be reviewed; and
there should be a critical reappraisal of the methods and supervision of organizations undertaking adoption.

30 McWHINNIE, ALEXINA M. (1968)

'Group counselling with 78 adoptive families', 2 parts, *Case Conference*, vol. 14, no. 11, pp. 407—12 and vol. 14, no. 12, pp. 456—8.
Groups were arranged for couples who had adopted children through the Guild of Service, Edinburgh, and the results noted and are here discussed. Variations were made in the age of the children, the make-up of the family, and by selection or non-selection according to the family circumstances. It was found that the groups were valued by the adopters, that there was advantage in selecting families with similar situations or problems, and that adopters with very disturbed problems of personality and relationship cannot be helped in this way. The content of the discussion groups, and the topics discussed are listed, and commented on.

31 NEELY, ALBERT (1969)

'Adoption by foster parents', *Child Welfare*, vol. 48, no. 3, pp. 163—4.
A review of the 92 adoptions arranged in one twelve-month period by the Children's Division of the Cook County Department of Public Welfare, of whom 52 were Negro or other race, and 38 white.

32 PEPPER, GERALD WESLEY (1967)

'Interracial adoptions: family profile, motivation and coping methods', *Dissertation Abstracts*, vol. 27 (8-A), p. 2621.
As a result of this study of 50 couples who in 1964 had adopted a child of mixed racial background (24) or a child of similar ethnic background (26) it was found: that those who adopted a child of mixed racial background seemed to be 'more eligible' applicants (judged by income and education), and their motives were a mixture of wanting a child and wanting to help a child; they coped with the role handicap by acknowledging the difference between themselves and the biological family.

33 PLATTS, H.K. (1970)

'Mothers seeking to relinquish children for adoption', *Children*, vol. 17, no. 1, pp. 27—30.

A study of over 1,000 cases by the Los Angeles County Department of Adoptions showed that social workers' impressions were wrong: e.g. that 40 per cent of the mothers had previously relinquished a child — the proportion was 9% — and that 20 per cent were married and living with their husband — the proportion was 5%. Other deductions were made about Mexican, Anglo and Negro mothers.

34 RAYNOR, LOIS (1971)

Giving up a baby for adoption, Association of British Adoption Agencies, 75 pp.

One hundred and twenty-four mothers from 27 hospitals were interviewed, and 81 were interviewed a second time from five to nine months later. It was found that many of the measures intended to help the mother come to a mature decision, and protect her rights as the mother of the child, were seen by the mothers themselves as a kind of punishment, in that it meant returning continually to the painful decision about giving up the child, — whichever way they decided. The desirability of shortening the time for coming to a decision and making it, dispensing with the guardian *ad litem* visit, are examples of the views expressed, — though there was wide variety in individual reactions.

35 REECE, SHIRLEY and LEVIN, BARBARA (1968)

'Psychiatric disturbances in adopted children: a descriptive study', *Social Work*, vol. 13, no. 1, pp. 101—11.

A report on a study of thirty adopted children referred to a psychiatric clinic in San Francisco over a period of ten years. The study was confined to non-relative adoptions, and excluded intrafamilial and step-parent adoptions. It is concluded that adopted children are not over-represented in psychiatric case-loads, but that they do show serious aggressive and anti-social symptoms, and there is some discussion of why this should be.

36 RIPPLE, LILIAN (1968)

'A follow-up study of adopted children', *Social Service Review*, vol 42, no. 4, pp. 479—99.

This investigation was made into the post-adoptive experiences of 160 children placed in infancy by the Illinois Children's Home and Aid Society, and who were seven to ten years old at the time of the investigation. Among the findings and conclusions are:
that 'good' parenting could not be predicted, but that a few major factors of 'bad' parenting can be identified;
lengthy investigation of suitability to adopt, and attempts to match children and adoptive parents, are not justified;
agencies should rather give more attention to what help applicants can be given to overcome difficulties

and short-comings, during the early months after placement.
Detailed comments by Mrs. Florence Kreech support the general conclusions.

37 SCHWARTZ, EDWARD M. (1967)

'A comparative study of some personality characteristics of adopted and non-adopted boys', *Dissertation Abstracts*, vol. 27 (7-B), pp. 2518—19.
As a result of this study of 25 adopted and 25 matched unadopted boys some eight to eleven years after their adoption, it was concluded that the adopted boys were more vulnerable to emotional and psychiatric problems, and that this was intensified because of parental anxieties, the child's need to know about his origins, and the problem of coping with the rejection by natural parents. Agencies gave parents too little help in working through their conflicts about adoption.

38 SCHWARTZ, EDWARD M. (1970)

'Family romance fantasy in children adopted in infancy', *Child Welfare*, vol. 49, no. 7, pp. 386—91.
A study of 25 matched boys adopted before the age of six months, with 25 boys not adopted, and living with both parents, showed that the family romance is of no greater significance for the adopted than for the non-adopted children.

39 SEGLOW, JEAN, KELLMER PRINGLE, M.L. and WEDGE, PETER (1972)

Growing Up Adopted. A long-term national study of adopted children and their families. National Foundation for Educational Research, 199 pp.
This research project is based on an intensive follow up of the 145 available adopted children who formed part of the cohort of children born in one week in 1958, and about whom very full information was available from the National Child Development Study, and from subsequent studies of this cohort (Kellmer Pringle, Butler and Davie 1966, and Davie, Butler and Goldstein 1972). Some of the significant findings include:
in all aspects of ability and attainment examined the adopted children did as well, or even better than, the other children in the cohort;
adopted children showed few overall differences in their behaviour and adjustment at school from those who were not adopted, but there was a markedly higher degree of 'maladjustment' among illegitimate children who remained with their natural mothers.
Suggestions based on the evidence of the research study are made for improving the services provided for the adoption of children.

40 SILVER, L.B. (1970)

'Frequency of adoption in children with the neurological learning disability syndrome', *Journal of Learning Disabilities*, vol. 3, pp. 306—10, bibl.
A study of 80 children with brain damage leading to neurologically-based learning disabilities. Ten of the children had been adopted, more than three times

26

the incidence of adoption in the general population. Exploration of the circumstances of the births were hampered because information was not available from the agencies concerned.

41 STARR, PHILIP, TAYLOR, DOLORES A. and TAFT, RUTH (1970)

'Early life experiences and adoptive parenting', *Social Casework*, vol. 51, no. 8, pp. 491—500.

The effect of early life experiences on performance as adoptive parents were examined in the case of 395 couples, in four significant areas: inconsistency in discipline, the 'telling process', experiencing developmental tasks as stressful, and using counselling services with family problems. In all cases the differences between the groups was minimal, and it was not possible to show that there is a positive association between the adoptive couple's early life experiences and their performance as parents.

42 TEC, LEON and GORDON, SUSANNE (1967)

'The adopted child's adaptation to adolescence'. *American Journal of Orthopsychiatry*, vol. 37, no. 2, p. 402.

The number of adopted children referred to a Child Guidance Centre in Connecticut was found to be larger than their ratio in the general population, and as a result of a study it was concluded that the problems of adolescence were exacerbated, for both children and parents, by adoption; including problems associated with 'Family Romance', resolution of the oedipal struggle, the 'Identity Crisis', and impulse control.

43 THOMAS, MORLAIS (1971)

'Foster/adoptive home breakdowns', *Child Adoption*, vol. 66, no. 4, pp. 28—33.

A study made of the 25 instances of breakdown of placements made in foster homes with a view to adoption out of the 735 placements made by the Church of England Children's Society in a four year period. Though not statistically significant, the reasons for breakdown are given as:
1. Foster/adoptive parents unable to accept child   14
2. Jealousy of foster/adoptive parents' own child   4
3. Mental and physical problems of foster child   3
4. Marital problems   2
5. Inability of extended family to accept the child 1
6. Illness of foster/adoptive mother   1

                                                    25

44. TRISELIOTIS, JOHN (1968)

'Courts and adoption practice', *Case Conference*, vol. 15, no. 5, pp. 190—7.

This study covered 923 adoptions legalized by 20 Sheriff Courts in Scotland in 1968 in the case of children placed by 12 agencies. The general conclusions were that too many individuals and agencies are involved in the adoption process, with a consequent weakening of the sense of responsibility of each. The role of the Curator is superfluous. Adoption petitions should be heard not in the Sheriff Courts but in the new Children's Panels.

45 TRISELIOTIS, JOHN
(1969)

'The timing of the single mother's decision in relation to adoption agency practice', *Child Adoption*, vol. 58, no. 3, pp. 29—39.

A study of 923 cases of adoption orders made by Sheriff Courts in Scotland, of the practice of twelve adoption agencies, and of 221 single mothers who gave birth to a child in a city hospital in 1965. The majority of the latter (72·9 per cent) kept to the decision they had made *before* the confinement, and changes in decision are listed and discussed, and the importance is stressed of adequate casework for the mother, and a flexible practice to meet individual needs.

46 WINGFIELD, F.
(1969)

'Prospective adopters' groups: an experiment', *Social Work* (Br.), vol. 26, no. 4, pp. 14—16.

A description of an experimental series of groups for prospective adopters arranged by the Devon County Children's Department as part of the selection procedure, but mainly 'for education towards the adoption situation'. Among the matters discussed are: number of meetings, size, order of introducing topics, and whether childless couples only.

SECTION II Policy and practice

47 ADVISORY COUNCIL ON CHILD CARE FOR ENGLAND AND WALES AND ADVISORY COUNCIL ON CHILD CARE FOR SCOTLAND (1970)

A guide to adoption practice, HMSO, 152 pp.

This handbook gives a comprehensive review of adoption practice in the United Kingdom for the guidance of the agencies concerned, and for others who wish to be informed about it. It examines areas of the present practice and the law, about which there is some misgiving, and which it recommends to the attention of the Houghton Committee. Among these matters are:

making the welfare of the child paramount in legal proceedings;

reconciliation of the provisions of the various relevant acts;

clarification of the law as it affects the putative father;

the possibility of grandparents and other relatives being able to apply for a form of legal guardianship as an alternative to adoption;

a review of the required arrangements for independent adoptions, and welfare supervision; the statutory functions of the guardian *ad litem*; the functions of case committees; the financial aspects of adoption; the required medical examinations; protection of a child for whom an adoption has been refused; a special court for hearing adoption applications; the central registration of adoption agencies.

48 ANDREWS, ROBERTA G. (1967)

'Quasi-adoption benefits negro children', *Child Welfare*, vol. 46, no. 1, p. 45.

Replies to Fowler ('The urban middle-class negro' q.v.) by quoting the experience of over 20 years quasi-adoption in Pennsylvania resulting in adoption in the case of some 20 per cent of long-term foster placements.

49 ANDREWS, ROBERTA G. (1968)

'Permanent placement of negro children through quasi-adoption', *Child Welfare*, vol. 47, no. 10, pp. 583—6, 613.

29

This article describes the formation of 'Families for Interracial Adoption' and the methods used to encourage the adoption of children of non-white or mixed racial origin. In two years, from 1967—69, 147 couples have adopted negro children, 30 oriental children, and 50 Indian children.

50 ANDREWS,
ROBERTA G. (1971)

'When is subsidized adoption preferable to long-term foster care?', *Social Service News*, vol. 1, no. 10, pp. 3—7. Also *Child Welfare*, vol. 50, no. 4, pp. 194—200.

This article examines the various arrangements made for subsidized adoption in the six states where it has been introduced, and summarizes the advantages and disadvantages of subsidized adoption and long-term foster care.

51 ANSFIELD, JOSEPH
G. (1971)

The adopted child. Charles C. Thomas, Springfield, Ill.

A psychiatrist, whose practice is mainly concerned with adolescents and young adults, discusses informally some of the matters that have come to his attention in the course of his work. His main plea is for flexibility (on the part of agencies and adopters, in being prepared to consider practices they are not accustomed to), and in particular for *not* telling a child he is adopted, particularly at an early age, unless the matter arises naturally.

52 ASSOCIATION OF
CHILD CARE OFFICERS
(1969)

Adoption — the way ahead. ACCO monograph No. 3, 87 pp.

A case is made out for a reform of the adoption legislation in the United Kingdom, based on oral and written evidence from professional sources.

Four criteria are suggested when deciding whether an adoption application should be brought to court:
(a) It must not create unnecessary confusion for a child in his relationships;
(b) It must not unnecessarily confuse a child's sense of identity;
(c) It must be the most appropriate way of securing a particular child's future;
(d) In each instance the child should be placed in a home which will meet his particular needs.

Five implications of these principles are stated:
(a) No child should be considered for adoption unless placed specifically for adoption by a registered agency;
(b) If an adoption order is inappropriate it should be possible to make a guardianship order;
(c) The standards of work of adoption agencies must be guaranteed by registration and inspection, and they must have access to a full range of child care facilities and resources;
(d) The present role and duties of the guardian *ad litem* would become superfluous;
(e) A mother's right to withdraw her consent to adoption must cease once the child has been placed.

Among the results of these proposals is the abolition of adoption by relatives, (including parents, and step-parents), and of direct and third party placements.
A number of detailed proposals are made.

53 BALL, G. (1970)

'The use of groups in the process of adoption', *Case Conference*, vol. 16, no. 10, pp. 406—8.

A description of the way in which a local authority adoption agency uses group discussion as part of the application process and again later on after the child has been placed in the adoptive home. The procedure is outlined, some of the values listed, and an excerpt is given from a group discussion by way of example.

54 BELCHER, GWEN (1970)

'Quest for a coloured baby', *Child Adoption*, vol. 60, no. 2, pp. 24—6.

Describes the difficulty encountered by an eligible couple, living some way from London, in finding a coloured baby to adopt, mainly, it would seem, because of distance from the agency bases.

55 BISKIND, S.E. (1966)

'Helping adoptive families meet the issues in adoption', *Child Welfare*, vol. 45, no. 3, pp. 145—50.

Describes what has been found out as a result of supplementing post-adoptive case-work with group counselling for adoptive parents, including some who have adopted children of other ethnic origins. Group discussion enriches the individual casework done with the family. Individual cases are quoted.

56 BISKIND, S.E., FINGER, S., SACKS, G.G. and SCHWARTZ, W. (1966)

'The group method with clients, foster families and adoptive families', *Child Welfare*, vol. 45, no. 10, pp. 561—75.

This symposium is made up of three papers and a discussion. The experience of using group methods for three groups of adoptive parents, for unmarried mothers and their parents, and for foster parents of pre-adoptive children respectively is presented, and an attempt made in the discussion paper to assess the reasons for the positive response of the participants to the group situation — the 'mutual aid' features — and the consequences for the agency and the practitioners involved — learning to 'help people to help one another'.

57 BRADEN, JOSEPHINE A. (1970)

'Adoption in a changing world', *Social Casework*, vol. 50, no. 8, pp. 486—90.

A discussion of what is claimed are significant changes which have occurred of recent years in the work of the adoption visitor in America, mainly in her relationship with applicants. The nature of this confrontation is analysed, and conclusions drawn about the implications for the supervisory and administrative framework for adoption agencies.

Adoption in Brief

58 BRANDON, JOAN
(1966)

'Voluntary adoption agencies and selection of adopters', *Case Conference*, vol. 13, no. 6, pp. 202—7.
A disappointingly small number (22) of British voluntary adoption agencies agreed to take part in the investigation here reported. Using the replies to a questionnaire, a summary is made of the adoption procedures of these agencies, with particular reference to the way they select families with whom they will place a child, and the criteria they rely on.

59 BRANHAM, E. (1970)

'One parent adoptions', *Children*, vol. 17, no. 3, pp. 103—7.
A report by the Los Angeles County Department of Adoptions of the placement of 36 'hard-to-place' children with a lone adopter, which is to be followed by a longitudinal study to evaluate results.

60 BRITISH
ASSOCIATION OF
SOCIAL WORKERS
(1971)

'Evidence to the Houghton Committee on Adoption', *Social Work Today*, vol. 2, no. 3, pp. 13—15.
The main comments of a BASW working party on the Houghton Committee's working paper (see Home Office 1970) are neatly summarized with a minimum of argument, and showing clearly the points of agreement and disagreement. Among the points agreed are: central registration of adoption agencies, third party and direct adoptions discontinued, guardian *ad litem* unnecessary, final parental consent to adoption to be given before the adoption hearing, adoption by natural parent abolished, 'guardianship' to be available to relatives and foster-parents.
Among the points of disagreement are: subsidized adoption, parental consent *automatically* dispensed with, six weeks period after birth before parental consent to adoption should not be reduced.

61 BURGESS, LINDA C.
(1968)

'The unmarried father in adoption planning', *Children*, vol. 15, no. 2, pp. 71—4.
Describes an experimental policy of a voluntary adoption society in Washington D.C. in insisting on access to the father of illegitimate children before arranging for their adoption. The policy resulted in a rising number of applicants, and information that made 'matching' more effective. The results for both mother and father are described, and appeared to be advantageous, although a full casework service for the fathers was not possible.

62 CARRILINE,
MADELINE M. (1970)

'Working with the Adoption Resource Exchange', in *Child Adoption*, vol. 61, no. 3, pp. 45—9.
A description of the work and purpose of the Adoption Resource Exchange, and a discussion of some of the matters that arise from it about the adoption of coloured children, and the casework involved.

32

63 CAVENAGH, WINIFRED and POST, ROSE (1971)

'Adoption procedure — views from the court', *Social Work Today*, vol. 1, no. 11, pp. 33—8.

A discussion of whether the welfare of the child should be paramount in deciding disputed adoptions, and the implications of this in general terms. Reference is made to the Houghton Committee working paper (Home Office 1970). The desirability of an earlier date for final parental consent is disputed, and the place of the guardian *ad litem* is defended.

64 CHAMBERS, D.E. (1970)

'Willingness to adopt atypical children', *Child Welfare*, vol. 49, pp. 275—9.

For this study group, willingness to adopt atypical children appears to be 'high' for children under five years of age, who are physically handicapped, are slow learners, or are of American Indian or Spanish-American parentage. ('Atypical' is used to mean 'hard-to-place' for the following reasons: physical handicap, age over five, American Indian, Spanish-American, Negro, emotional disturbance, mental retardation).

65 CHAPPELAAR, EDITH M. and FRIED, JOYCE (1967)

'Helping adopting couples come to grips with their new parental roles', *Children*, vol. 14, no. 6, pp. 223—6.

Describes a four-year programme of group meetings for adoptive parents during the immediate post-placement period, supplementary to the caseworker's home visits, and the value found in them — mainly in enabling the parents to talk about their initial difficulties of adjustment.

66 CHEMA, REGINA et al. (1970)

'Adoptive placement of the older child', *Child Welfare*, vol. 49, no. 8, pp. 450—8.

Describes the experience of a team of adoption workers, covering between them 20 years of adoption work, of the difficulties in placing the 'older child' (defined here as 'more than two years old'). The subject is dealt with under the headings: *Separation* from natural parents, siblings, and foster parents; *Placement Techniques and Procedures* with the adoptive parents, the foster parents, and the child; and *Post-adoptive Supervision.*

67 CHILD ADOPTION (1968)

'Adoption at the crossroads', *Child Adoption*, vol. 54, pp. 27—9.

A report of an 'Adoption Workshop' at Exeter in July 1967, led by Professor and Mrs. David Kirk, in which a good deal of emphasis was placed on the need for all parties to learn their role in adoption, and not pretend it is the same as in a natural family.

68 CHILD ADOPTION (1970)

'Adoption in New South Wales 1968/69', *Child Adoption*, vol. 42, no. 4, pp. 45—7.

Gives particulars from the Annual Report of the New South Wales Child Welfare Department about the 1,345 adoption orders made during the year

1968—9. The number of babies placed was 1,675 and the number of applicant couples was 1,882. Tables set out the ages and race of children adopted and the ages and religions of the adoptive parents.

69 CHILD ADOPTION
(1970)

'Adoption in New Zealand', *Child Adoption*, vol. 60, no. 2, pp. 41—2.

Information culled from several sources giving the experiences of running educational classes for prospective adopters, statistical facts about adoption in New Zealand, and what is called the 'mopokuna' (grandchild) syndrome. The latter refers to a Maori custom of placing a child with grandparents, whose own children have grown up and moved elsewhere, and is part of the Maori extended family system. It mentions the difficulty a 'mopokuna' finds in returning to his own family later on, if the circumstances arise, particularly at adolescence. Finally there is reference to the high legal and other costs which may be impeding adoption in New Zealand.

70 CHILD ADOPTION
(1970)

'Adoption in Northern Ireland', *Child Adoption*, vol. 61, no. 3, pp. 21—2.

A brief commentary on the Adoption Act 1967 of Northern Ireland, and the rules made under it, pointing out any variations, none of them of great importance, from the English law.

71 COSTIN, LELA B.
(1970)

'Adoption of children by single parents', *Child Adoption*, vol. 59, no. 1, pp. 31—3.

A discussion of the use of placement of children with single parents for adoption, and the limited experience of it in the United States — usually for 'hard-to-place' children.

72 DILLOW, LOUISE B.
(1968)

'The group process in adoptive homefinding', *Children*, vol. 15, no. 4, pp. 153—7.

A report of the experiences of two agencies in using group methods as part of the home study prior to an adoption placement. They were found useful, not in saving caseworkers' time, but in improving the content of the home studies, and in reducing the applicants' anxiety.

73 EDGAR, MARGARET
(1971)

'The group approach in Canada', *Child Adoption*, vol. 65, no. 3, pp. 19—21.

Describes the use made by the Open Door Society, Montreal, of 'intake groups', and 'adoption preparation groups' for adopting parents, the ground covered and the useful purposes they serve.

74 EPSTEIN, LAURA and HEYMANN, IRMGARD (1967)

'Some decisive processes in adoption planning for older children', *Child Welfare*, vol. 46, no. 1, pp. 5—9.

A single case is described fully to illustrate the policy and methods advocated by the Child and Family Services of Chicago, based on a five-year experiment, to achieve adoption of older children rather than their long-term foster care.

75 FISCHER,
CLARENCE D. (1971)

'Gallagher: the black experience', *Children*, vol. 18, no. 3, p. 119.

Gives the experience of an organisation called 'Homes for black children' in finding black adopters. There is no difficulty in recruitment because the agency is clearly black, not white.

76 FISCHER,
CLARENCE D. (1971)

'Homes for black children', *Child Welfare*, vol. 50, no. 2, pp. 108—11.

An account of a special adoption programme to recruit adoptive homes for black children. One hundred and thirty-five black children were placed in under 14 months, all but one with non-white families.

77 FOWLER, IRVING A. (1966)

'The urban middle-class negro and adoption', *Child Welfare*, vol. 45, no. 9, p. 522.

This report of studies in Buffalo and Rochester, New York, supports the findings of Deasy and Quinn 1962 (*Child Welfare*, vol. 46, pp. 400—7) that efforts to persuade childless middle-class Negro couples to adopt are unlikely to produce massive results. The best suggestion for achieving substantial results is to provide financial assistance for significant periods of time to experienced parents of working, lower middle-class status.

78 GALLAGHER,
URSULA M. (1968)

'The adoption of mentally retarded children', *Children*, vol. 15, no. 1, pp. 17—21.

A case is stated for the adoption of mildly retarded children, and some principles are laid down, based on the limited experience of the writer, and quoting some of the cases known to her.

79 GALLAGHER,
URSULA M. (1971)

'Black and white', *Children*, vol. 18, no. 4, p. 160.

Reply to points raised by Kahn (q.v.) about black children adopted by white families.

80 GALLAGHER,
URSULA M. (1971)

'Adoption resources for black children', *Children*, vol. 18, no. 2, pp. 49—53.

A summary of the information available from various studies of the factors involved in increasing the number of adoptive homes for black children in America by trans-racial adoption and by increasing the number of black families who will adopt black children.

81 GEBBETT, STEPHEN H. (1971)

'A home for a child not a child for a home. An enquiry into aspects of the administrative framework of adoptive services in England and Wales', *Child Adoption*, vol. 63, no. 1, pp. 37—55.

This wide examination of administrative procedures is based on a work-group of practitioners and on work with two agencies, one voluntary and one statutory, and examines selection methods and rules for prospective adopters. Excess of applicants tended to make selection practices into principles, and made the 'Kirk hypothesis' of 'self-selection' out of the question for a large society. Myths connected with the influence of heredity are discussed, the make-up and shortcomings of case-committees examined, placement and supervision arrangements reviewed, and the place of the probation officer as guardian *ad litem*, and the problem of 'snatch-back'. Reflections on the national situation are towards national registration by the central government, and regional organisation of the service. Considerable attention is given to costs and finance, and some speculations are indulged in about the future supply and demand of babies.

82 GENTILE, ANGELA (1970)

'Subsidized adoption in New York: how the law works — some problems', *Child Welfare*, vol. 49, no. 10, pp. 576—80.

Describes the provisions of the New York State adoption subsidy law of 1968, and its limitations; the ways in which it is being implemented; and some difficulties that have been discovered. By the end of December 1969, 183 requests had been made, and 37 adoptions had been arranged, mainly negro and some Puerto Rican.

83 GILL, D.G. (1969)

'Illegitimacy and adoption', *Child Adoption*, vol. 56, no. 1, pp. 25—37.

An examination of the illegitimacy figures from 1955—1965, and the changing pattern in the incidence of illegitimate births associated with youth, urban living and sophistication rather than with rural life, poverty and family disorganisation. The figures for illegitimate births in Aberdeen in the three main categories are:

women cohabitating	25·3 per cent
women 'ever married' (i.e. married, separated, widowed or divorced)	15·5 per cent
single women	59·2 per cent

When the numbers of children adopted are considered it was found that the factor most significant in distinguishing the mothers who kept and those who released their children for adoption was their social class.

84 GOLDBERG, HARRIET L. AND LINDE, LLEWELLYN H. (1969)

'The case for subsidized adoption', *Child Welfare*, vol. 48, no. 2, pp. 96—9.

Some discussion of subsidized adoptions following their legalization in New York State, the first in U.S.A.

85 GOOD, JAMES (1970)

'A Cork society's adoption survey', *Child Adoption*, vol. 60, no. 2, pp. 31—4.

A survey of the 641 children whose adoption had been arranged over a ten year period, 1954—1964, by the St. Anne's Adoption Society. The main type of information resulting is a count of the incidence of certain sorts of difficulty, such as poor intelligence, physical and emotional ill-health, serious behaviour problems, telling the child about his adoption. The difficulties reported are remarkably few as a whole. Other matters mentioned by a few of the respondents were the absence of godparents' names from baptismal certificates, lack of information about the child's history before adoption, and the length of the trial adoption period.

86 GRIFFIN, B.P. and ARFFA, M.S. (1970)

'Recruiting adoptive homes for minority children; one approach', *Child Welfare*, vol. 49, pp. 105—7.

A description of a programme undertaken by the New England Home for Little Wanderers to promote interracial adoptions by both white and black families. In 1967 'Families for Interracial Adoption' was formed with 32 families, and had grown to 400 families in two years. The purposes and programme are described and briefly discussed.

87 HARTLEY, P. (1970)

'Group education to assist in adoption assessment', *Child Adoption*, vol. 60, no. 2, pp. 17—23.

An initial report of a limited scheme of 'self-selection' of couples applying to adopt a child, by means of group discussion. The only pre-selection is the completion of medicals and a discussion with any couples whose medical report is unsatisfactory, with a view to their withdrawal. The content and structure of the nine discussion sessions are described, and some of the conclusions arrived at after eighteen months working.

88 HEWITT, JOAN (1967)

'Approaches to the selection of adopters', *Accord*, vol. 12, no. 1, pp. 12—15.

Reflections of an experienced adoption visitor of a voluntary agency, listing the matters she has found most important, and concluding that the *attitudes* of the adopters (toward each other, towards childlessness and towards the natural mother) are the most important of all.

89 HOME OFFICE (1970)

The Adoption of Children. Working Paper of the Departmental Committee on the Adoption of Children. HMSO, 192 pp.

This working paper contains the provisional proposals of the Committee on which the comments of interested parties are invited. Among the main propositions are:
a nationally available adoption service as an integral part of the social work service;
registration of voluntary adoption agencies should become a central government responsibility;
placement with non-relatives to be confined to registered adoption agencies;
adoption of a child by his own natural parent to be

abolished, and by a step-parent only of spouse's illegitimate offspring;
'guardianship' should be made available to relatives and foster-parents already caring for the child;
the guardian *ad litem* should eventually disappear in agency cases, but be invoked in non-agency cases at the discretion of the court;
parental consent to adoption should become final at a time prior to the adoption hearing; and the minimum period of six weeks for the mother's consent should be reduced;
the involvement of the putative father in the planning of the child's future should be encouraged, and his position in law should be clarified;
there should be a unified family jurisdiction (a family court) covering adoption, guardianship and affiliation proceedings, and ultimately all juvenile court matters;
in England and Wales, access to original birth records should only be granted by permission of the court;
the requirements for medical examination and the functions of adoption committees should be regularized.

90 HOME OFFICE
(1972)

The Adoption of Children. Report of the Departmental Committee on the Adoption of Children. HMSO, 135 pp.
    Among the most important of the recommendations, some of which require new legislations, are:
local authorities should have a legal duty to provide an adoption service;
voluntary adoption agencies should be required to register with the Secretary of State;
no adoption of a child by a non-relative save through a registered agency;
pilot schemes of payment of allowances to adopters should be legalized;
a form of guardianship should be made available to relatives and foster-parents;
the law on the assumption or relinquishment of parental rights to be tidied up, and transfer of parental rights by a court for the purpose of adoption should be irrevocable;
first consideration should be given to the long-term welfare of the child in deciding whether parental consent to adoption is being unreasonably withheld;
welfare supervision of a child by the local authority after placement for adoption should cease;
an adopted person of eighteen or over should be entitled to a copy of his original birth certificate.

91 JOHNS, RUTH I.
(1970)

'Non-institutional accommodation for mother and baby', *Child Adoption*, vol. 61, no. 3, pp. 39—44.
    This article describes the work of the Family First Trust of Nottingham to provide accommodation, and therefore a genuine choice, for unsupported mothers who have to consider whether to consent to their baby's adoption, or attempt to keep him. The Trust

interviews 250 unsupported mothers each year, and provides at 'The Croft' bed-sitters with kitchen recesses for nine mothers, plus a resident warden and family (Mrs. Johns herself).

92 JONES, MARY (1966)

'I said goodbye to my baby', *Mental Health*, vol. 25, no. 4, pp. 15—16.

A description by an unmarried mother of the process of deciding to agree to her baby being adopted and the various steps in the adoption procedure seen from her point of view.

93 KAHN, ROGER (1971)

'Black and white', *Children*, vol. 18, no. 4, p. 160.

Discusses some of the implications for a black child of being adopted by a white family (arising out of Gallagher's 'Adoption Resources for Black Children', *Children*, vol. 18, no. 2).

94 KAREH, DIANA (1970)

Adoption and the coloured child. Epworth Press, ix, 130 pp.

Assembles information from many sources to support the contention that there are a large number of coloured children (many in care) who are available for adoption, but that social worker time is short for the requirements, and that the Adoption Resources Exchange (see Raynor) would go some way towards bringing adopters and children together.

95 KASPROWICZ, ALFRED L. (1967)

'Interpreting rejection to adoptive applicants', Ch. 12 in Younghusband, E. (Ed.) *Social Work and Social Values.* Allen & Unwin.

A discussion of the importance of telling rejected applicants for adoption why they have been rejected, and of giving them a chance to come to terms with their rejection by group meetings, interview and interpretation. Three examples are given and discussed.

96 LAMBERT, LYDIA (1971)

'Adoption: the statistical picture 1970', *Child Adoption*, vol. 63, no. 1, pp. 11—22.

An examination of the numbers of children placed for adoption in England and Wales in the years 1966/7/8/9.

97 LANSBERRY, CHARLES (1969)

'A major question in subsidized adoption', *Child Welfare*, vol. 43, no. 8, pp. 499—500.

A brief discussion of whether casework services should be provided when a subsidy is paid. A case against is stated in this letter, and replied to by Goldberg and Llewellyn (q.v.)

98 LAWDER, ELIZABETH A. (1966)

'Quasi-adoption', *Children*, vol. 13, pp. 11—12.*

*Entries marked with an asterisk (*) are not annotated. The articles were not available for consultation at the time of going to press, but the entries have been included for the sake of completeness.

99 LAWDER, ELIZABETH A. *et al.* (1971)	'A study of black adoption families: a comparison of a traditional and a quasi-adoption program'. *Child Welfare League of America*, 77 pp. A description and study of a service set up in 1964 by the Children's Aid Society of Pennsylvania to provide stable and permanent homes for the considerable numbers of black children needing them. It was found that there were a group of negro families interested in providing a foster home but deterred from contemplating adoption by financial uncertainty and anxiety about legal responsibility for the child.
100 LEEDING, A.E. (1970)	'Group meetings with prospective adopters. A county council experiment', *Child Adoption*, vol. 59, no. 1, pp. 39—41. A description of the experience of the Warwickshire County Council in arranging group meetings for applicants for a child for adoption. Originally undertaken to save time by giving initial information to several couples at one time, it was found to have positive values, and has been persisted with, and serves among other things as a self-selection process, since some couples withdraw of their own accord, instead of having to be 'rejected'. Figures are given for a twelve-month period.
101 McWHINNIE, ALEXINA M. (1971)	'Foster care *v.* residential nursery for the child awaiting adoption or assessment for adoption', *Child Adoption*, vol. 64, no. 2, pp. 16—18. An informed summary of the pros and cons of a child being cared for in a residential nursery or in a foster home while awaiting placement for adoption.
102 MADISON, BERNICE and SCHAPIRO, MICHAEL (1969)	'Long-term foster family care: what is its potential for minority group children?', *Public Welfare*, vol. XXVII, no. 2, pp. 167—91. A thorough-going study of some 1,200 children, mainly negro, accepted over a four year period for long-term foster care. As a result some were in fact adopted by the foster-parents, or by other adoptive parents, and some were returned to their homes. Very few were transferred to institutional care. The project showed that these 'minority' group children could be found homes in babyhood and infancy, and that the majority resulted in stable long-term placements.
103 MIDDELSTADT, E., KENYON, E., STAHLKE, R.D. and MATZE, F.A. (1970)	'Adoption counselling—a new opportunity for growth', *Child Adoption*, vol. 62, no. 4, pp. 17—26 (reprinted from *Child Welfare*, vol. 46, no. 7, pp. 365—7, 385). This article, first published in 1967, describes the use of group interviews and group counselling to prepare couples for adoption when the number of children available exceeded the number of applicants to adopt. The situation has changed dramatically since then, so that the ratio is reversed. As the Editor of *Child Adoption* points out in a special note, the problem today is to provide what is needed by couples who will be disappointed and childless.

104 MONDLOH,
RAYMOND (1969)

'Changing practice in the adoptive home study, *Child Welfare*, vol. 48, no. 3, pp. 148—56.

The Minnesota Department of Public Welfare undertook a thorough review of its basic attitude and purposes in adoption and the effect on procedures for home study. Their work is directed towards knowing and helping couples to deepen their knowledge in four major areas; understanding and acceptance of adoption, child-rearing aptitude, emotional maturity, and marital adjustment.

105 NATIONAL
CHILDREN'S HOME
(1968)

'Residential nurseries and adoption practice', *Child Adoption*, vol. 54, pp. 43—6.

A reasoned statement of the practice of receiving babies offered for adoption into residential nurseries before placement in adoptive homes. (Ref. commentary on this article, 109).

106 PARFIT, JESSIE
(1971)

Spotlight on group work with parents in special circumstances. National Children's Bureau, 152 pp.

The first of five chapters is about 'Groups for adoptive parents' and gives first of all a short overview of the main points and trends. This is followed by short statements of the use made of groups for adoptive parents by ten local authorities and three voluntary agencies, and abstracts of chapters, articles and one book on the same topic. It is clear that groups are becoming a regular method of education and 'self-selection' for applicants to adopt children, in this country as well as in America, and that some experience is being assembled of group work with adopters at other stages, during and after placement of a child.

107 POLK, MARY
(1970)

'Maryland's programme of subsidized adoptions', *Child Welfare*, vol. 49, no. 10, pp. 581—3.

Describes the three-year struggle to establish the system of subsidized adoption as part of the foster-care programme. Payments are within 75 per cent of the foster care scale, and may be for a short term, or until the child is 21. Its value is in giving stable adoptive status to negro children who would otherwise remain as foster children. The same system has been used for crippled children. It was too early to assess the values of the scheme.

108 RATHBUN,
CONSTANCE and
KOLODNY, RALPH L.
(1967)

'A group-work approach in cross-cultural adoptions', *Children*, vol. 14, no. 3, pp. 117—21.

A description of a long-term programme of group meetings for couples who had adopted Chinese children. Procedures are described, and it is concluded that the meetings were valuable, but conclusions are treated with caution until a follow-up study has confirmed them.

41

109 REID, BARBARA C. 'Residential nurseries and adoption practice', *Child*
and HOOKER, J.N. *Adoption*, vol. 55, pp. 21—4.
(1968)   Two informed, critical comments from a local
authority and a voluntary agency on the article
(National Children's Home 1968, see 105) dealing
with the use of residential nurseries for receiving
babies prior to placement for adoption.

110 RICHARDS, 'The activities of the guardian *ad litem*', *Child Adop-*
KIRSTINE (1971) *tion*, vol. 66, no. 4, pp. 41—2.
A note of some of the things that can cause dis-
tress, and even unnecessary offence, when statutory
visits are made to prospective adopters and to their
referees.

111 ROSS, SHIRLEY R. 'A slighted resource', *Children*, vol. 18, no. 3, pp.
(1971)   119—20.
Refers to Gallagher's article ('Adoption resources
for black children', *Children*, vol. 18, no. 2) and urges
that more attention should be given to subsidizing the
adoption of black children to enable more black
families to provide homes for black children.

112 RUNSWICK, 'Classes for adoptive mothers', *Child Adoption*, vol.
HARRIET (1969) 56, no. 1, pp. 43—4.
A syllabus is given of a short course of three
classes, each of two-and-a-half or three hours to pre-
pare women who are about to adopt babies, for the
arrival of their child. As the result of experience the
course was extended to mothers who were to receive
a second baby in their family.

113 SIMON, E. (1969) 'The selecting of adopters', *Mother and Child*, vol. 41,
no. 6, pp. 18—20.
A summary of a day conference of the Medical
Group of the Standing Conference of Societies Registered for Adoption, and of papers given by Mrs.
Kirstine Richards about methods of selecting adopters, by Dr. John Marshall on the doctor's role in
adoption, by Dr. Margaret Jackson giving the point of
view of those arranging third party adoptions, and
accounts by three adopters who had had unusual experiences.

114 SOCIAL SERVICE 'Expanding adoption resources', *Social Service Review*,
REVIEW (1968) vol. 42, no. 2, pp. 269—70.
Reference is made to Lawder's 'Quasi-adoption'
(q.v.) and the use of long-term foster-care for some
children needing adoption homes, and urges the
wider consideration and use of subsidies to make
more adoptive families available.

115 STANDING *Adoption societies practice*. 3rd ed., 11 pp.
CONFERENCE OF   A summary of answers by member societies to a
SOCIETIES series of 19 questions about their practice on the
REGISTERED FOR following matters: religion, marital status, age and
ADOPTION (1969) infertility of applicants, categories of children accep-
ted for adoption, and placing with overseas applicants.

42

116 SWAN, CLARA J. (1968)

'Adoption resource exchange', *Child Welfare*, vol. 47, no. 1, pp. 4—5.

Announces the formation of ARENA (The Adoption Resource Exchange of North America) and describes its purpose and importance.

117 TIZARD, BARBARA and JOSEPH, ANNE (1970)

'Today's foundlings', *New Society*, no. 418, pp. 584—5.

An exploration of what had happened five years later to 3,055 children under five admitted to the care of three large voluntary societies during the years 1962—4. A quarter of all the children were living in institutions (40 per cent of the coloured boys), 46 per cent had been restored to a relation and 18 per cent had been adopted (the survey did not include those admitted specifically for adoption). The effect of sex and race on these figures is studied.

118 TRISELIOTIS, JOHN (1970)

Evaluation of adoption policy and practice. University of Edinburgh Press, 140 pp.

A descriptive study of a sample of 1,030 adoptions made in Scotland in 1965 in 20 Sheriff Courts, and of eight local authority and four voluntary adoption agencies and the 376 children placed by these agencies in the same year. In addition, material from a postal questionnaire, covering 38 local authority and four voluntary agencies were studied.

The general conclusions included the following points:

most adoption practice is very narrowly based and few agencies have formulated the principles on which they work;

the number of different people involved in the adoption process reduces the real responsibility felt by any one of them (because each assumed that someone else had done, or would do, what was necessary) and the number should be limited;

services to unmarried mothers, and adoption services, should be provided within the same agency;

explicit provision for local authority grants to be made to voluntary agencies should be arranged;

there should be clarification of the respective role of the case committees and professional adoption workers, what is meant by a 'fit' person, and what are the criteria of eligibility of applicants for adoption;

local authority agencies should be subject to the same regulations as voluntary ones; and some body other than the local authority should be responsible for registering and inspecting adoption agencies;

local authorities should be given powers to subsidize certain types of guardianship adoptions;

medical certificates on adopters should be obtained *before* the placement of a child;

there is urgent need for clarification of the concept of the 'welfare of the child';

the consent of the mother to the adoption of her

child should be possible at an earlier date — to be made final within a specified time-span; effective casework with the mother while her consent is being decided is needed; statutory post-placement supervision seems to have little value, if the standards of placing agencies are brought up to a proper level; the role of the curator *ad litem* should either be strengthened or abolished; consideration might be given to adoption cases being dealt with by the new Children's Hearings; adoption of children by relatives should be looked at again, (since their advantages to the child are doubtful, and the method involves an unacceptable secrecy and evasion); a duty should be placed on local authorities to provide adoption services, and services to unmarried mothers in general.

119 WATSON, KENNETH (1972)

'Subsidized adoption — a crucial investment', *Social Service News*, vol. 2, no. 11, pp. 11—16.

A description of subsidized adoption in seven American States and one voluntary agency. It summarizes the underlying assumptions, gives some indication of the numbers involved from the few statistics available, and cites a small selection of case examples. Some of the most common objections are listed, together with factors that impede more being done, even where legislation makes it permissible.

120 WHEELER, K.B. (1969)

'The use of adoptive subsidies', *Child Welfare*, vol. 48, no. 9, pp. 557—9.

This article summarizes the circumstances in which a family of five siblings ranging in age from four to ten years, with a background of severe deprivation, were placed with a couple in 1962, and in 1965 the adoption order was made. The placement was only possible as a result of a subsidy of 250 dollars a month paid by the placing agency to the adopters for six years. The experiment was an unqualified success, and the agency has begun to use a variety of subsidy arrangements, including:

(1) waiving of adoptive fees;
(2) payment of full boarding rate for stipulated period;
(3) payment of partial boarding rate for a stipulated period and
(4) payment of clothing and medical allowances — or a combination of more than one of these.

The agency's view on the use of subsidies can be summarized thus:

If, through the usual adoptive procedures, a permanent home cannot be obtained for a child, and the only barrier is economic, the agency will undertake to remove that barrier.

121 YOUNG, JOYCE
(1971)

'The adoption agency and the adopted person',
Child Adoption, vol. 66, no. 4, pp. 21—8.
Illustrates from particular instances the experience of Dr. Barnardo's in meeting the requests of
teenagers and adults, who have been adopted, abou:
their natural parents. A counselling service could help
both adopted and adopters.

SECTION III   Legal and medical matters

122 ASSOCIATION OF BRITISH ADOPTION AGENCIES (1970)

Medical Group Papers II, *Genetic and Psychological Aspects of Adoption*, 114 pp. (C).

The first part of this publication is a report of a day conference of the Medical Group of the Standing Conference of Societies Registered for Adoption in 1968 with the general title 'Genetic and Psychological Aspects of Adoption'. There are papers by Michael Humphrey on 'The need for parenthood', by Dr. Alexina McWhinnie on 'The attributes of well-adjusted adoptive parents', by Dr. Cedric Carter on 'Genetic considerations in adoption', by Dr. Michael Rutter on 'Psychological development: predictions from infancy' and by Professor Ronald Illingworth on 'Assessment for adoption'.

The second part is an account of a similar conference in 1969, and includes papers on 'Selecting Adopters' by Kirstine Richards, Dr. John Marshall, Dr. Margaret Jackson, the views of three adopters; and also a lecture by Dr. H. David Kirk entitled 'The selection of adopters — questions regarding authority and reasoning' (see Simon 1969, in *Mother and Child*, which is an account of the same conference).

123 BAMFORD, F.N. (1971)

'Medical forms for use in adoption', *Medical Officer*, vol. 125, no. 1, no. 3257, pp. 8—9.

Refers to the new revised set of standard forms for recording the results of medical examinations of both children and applicants prior to adoption. They have been produced by the Medical Group of the Association of British Adoption Agencies. The value of such examinations is discussed, and the use of the new forms is recommended.

124 BLOM-COOPER, LOUIS (1968)

'Parental rights in adoption cases. A new approach to the law of adoption', *Child Adoption*, vol. 54, pp. 19—25.

A discussion of the way in which the rights of those concerned are protected — particularly those of

46

the child — in the present procedures, and whether direct and third party adoptions should be made illegal. It is argued that reform is needed with, preferably, a 'family court', and only intervening in what would be an administrative registration, in matters of dispute, e.g. the withholding of parental consent. The object of the proposal is to ensure the child's best interests, and guarantee at the same time that parental rights are safeguarded.

125 CHILD ADOPTION (1967)

'Adoption Overseas — Australia', *Child Adoption*, vol. 51, pp. 40—2.

Some notes on the working of the present adoption laws in New South Wales, Victoria and South Australia

126 CHILD ADOPTION (1968)

'A new Greek adoption law', *Child Adoption*, vol. 55, pp. 31—2.

Among the provisions of the Greek amending Law 4532, 'On the adoption of minors under 18 years' (1966) are:
a report from a competent service or organization is required;
parental consent is inadmissible till child is three months old;
minimum age of adopters reduced from 50 to 35;
adoption inadmissible if adopters have a legitimate descendant, unless descendant is suffering from an incurable disease;
second adoptions allowed at court's discretion.

127 CHILD ADOPTION (1969)

'New French Law on Adoption', *Child Adoption*, vol. 56, no. 1, pp. 17—21.

This account of the French Adoption Bill, 1966, reflects the different history and philosophy of adoption in France. Among the points that catch the attention are:
that a child is not placed until three months after the giving of parental consent, and that children under two may only be placed through a recognized adoption agency;
that single persons as well as 'anybody over 35' may adopt;
that parental consent may be dispensed with if the child has been left 'in care' for more than a year;
and that people with their own children are not eligible for 'plenary' adoption.

128 CHILD ADOPTION (1969)

'Italy's new adoption law', *Child Adoption*, vol. 53, no. 1, p. 21.

A brief note of some of the provisions of the Law of 1967, by which the minimum age for adopters is dropped from 50 to 35, and successive adoptions by the same couple are now possible.

Adoption in Brief

129 CHILD ADOPTION
(1970)

'Changes in West Australian Adoption Law', *Child Adoption*, vol. 62, no. 4, p. 47.
Short notes on the effect of the Adoption of Children Amendment Act, 1964, which came into force in May 1970. The Child Welfare Department becomes the guardian of a child during adoption proceedings. If a mother wishes to revoke her consent to the child's adoption she must do so in writing within 30 days of signing the original consent.

130 COOPER,
CHRISTINE (1968)

'Medical practice in adoption agencies', *Child Adoption*, vol. 53, pp. 42—50.
On the basis of replies to a questionnaire to adoption agencies and local authorities, a comparison is made between the practice of the agencies and the local authorities on matters such as the number of doctors who advise the agency; what doctor examines the applicants and babies, and who assesses the medical forms; whether the doctor sees the applicants about the baby before placement, or three months after placement; whether a doctor sits on the case committee; and whether the agency runs a post-adoption counselling service. A number of recommendations are made, including the assessment of the medical reports on applicants by a consultant physician, and the use of standard medical forms.

131 DE LA CRUZ, F.F.
(1969)

'The high-risk infant; implications in adoption', *Clinical Paediatrics*, vol. 8, no. 9, pp. 516—25.
Starting from a calculation that mental retardation occurred among children in adoption service four times as frequently as in the general population, a study was made to ascertain what were the causes of the retardation, how they could be diagnosed early, and treated. The desirability of not waiting too long before making an adoption placement is pointed out.

132 FORFAR, J.O.
(1969)

'The role of the paediatrician in adoption medical practice', *Lancet*, vol. 1, no. 7607, pp. 1201—3.
It is argued in this article that the paediatrician can play an important and valuable role in adoption by advising about children who have some defect, in preventing their rejection out of hand, in advising prospective adopters what a child's needs will be, and in educating practitioners who propose to undertake adoption examinations.

133 FORFAR, J.O.
(1969)

'Worth and need in medico-social assessment: the adoption situation', *Child Adoption*, vol. 57, no. 2, pp. 25—34.
An examination of the nature and difficulties of the assessment of children offered for adoption and of prospective adopters, and the need for close co-operation between medical practitioners and social workers so as to integrate the assessment service that can be given.

Legal and medical matters

134 FRIDMAN, G.H.L. (1966)

'Foreign adoptions', *Child Care News*, no. 55, pp. 14—18.

The first of three articles reprinted from the *New Law Journal*, citing English appeal cases in which matters of inheritance and succession are in issue concerning children adopted in other countries (see Fridman 1967 and 1968).

135 FRIDMAN, G.H.L. (1967 and 1968)

'Foreign Adoptions', *Child Adoption*, vol. 52, pp. 19—24, vol. 53, pp. 21—4.

These two articles discuss on the basis of appeal judgements in English courts the difficulties arising in testamentary matters when one of the parties has been adopted in another country. The wide differences in the law in different countries make it difficult to be sure that an 'adoption' in one country will be recognized in another. Cases of custody and maintenance are also dealt with.

136 GOOD, JAMES (1971)

'Legal adoption in Ireland', *Child Adoption*, vol. 65, no. 3, pp. 23—7.

A commentary on some aspects of the law of adoption in Ireland, (dating from the first Adoption Act, 1952) and mentioning among other matters:
the mother cannot sign a consent until the baby is *over six months* old;
the legal exclusion of couples who have made a mixed marriage (Catholic, non-Catholic) from adopting;
no legal requirement to notify the authorities of the placement of a child, until an application is made for his adoption;
the law is administered, not by the courts, but by an Adoption Board;
delay in completing the adoption procedures after the application has been made — for months, or even years;
unsatisfactory home visiting system;
inadequacy of the baptismal certificate.

137 JAMIESON, G.K. (1967)

'Psychiatric disorders in adopted children', *Texas Medicine*, vol. 63, pp. 83—8.*

138 KENNY, T., BALDWIN, R. and MACKIE, J.B. (1967)

'Incidence of minimal brain injury in adopted children', *Child Welfare*, vol. 46, no. 1, pp. 24—9.

A review of case records over 12 years showed that a disproportionate incidence of adopted children had been referred. It seemed from the information available in a pilot study of 1,000 cases that the damage was due to injury sustained pre-natally or at birth, a factor allied to low socio-economic class, and that the damage was not corrected by the more generous life circumstances in an adopted family.

139 KNIGHT, IRIS G. (1971)

'Medical Confidentiality', *Child Adoption*, vol. 66, no. 4, pp. 7—11.

A doctor working with a large voluntary society

gives her personal views about the kind of information that must be treated as confidential, and how nevertheless to meet the proper requirements of the expanded social services. Most of the examples concern adoption situations.

140 KORNITZER, MARGARET (1969)

'Does adoption law need redrafting?', *Municipal Journal*, vol. 77, no. 23, p. 1424.
A discussion of some of the things that are thought to need changing in the law as it stands in the U.K. including — the rights of long-stay foster parents, the respective virtues of foster care and adoption, the courts' power to dispense with parental consent to adoption, the French pattern of *adoption simple*, and the American pattern of subsidized adoption.

141 MACLAY, DAVID T. (1969)

'The children's psychiatrist in court cases concerning adoption', *Child Adoption*, vol. 57, no. 2, pp. 35—8.
A short consideration of the part a psychiatrist can play in court cases concerning adoption, custody, and other matters, how unnecessary conflict between expert evidence can be avoided, and quoting particular examples by way of illustration.

142 MEYER, B. (1970)

'Les conditions juridiques de l'adoption', *Gazette Medicale de France*, vol. 77, no. 29, pp. 6069—74.
A summary of the main provisions of the French adoption law of 11 July 1966, explaining the difference between 'simple adoption' and 'full adoption'. The former is equivalent to a legally protected foster-care situation.

143 MICHAELS, NAOMI (1966)

'The historical development of the law of custody and adoption', *Child Adoption*, vol. 50, pp. 25—36.
A review of the development of the law of custody and adoption in this country, and the principles underlying it. Special attention is given to the rights of natural parents, the giving and withholding of consents, and the significance of the so-called 'blood-tie' case.

144 OFFORD, D.R., APONTE, J.F. and CROSS, L.A. (1969)

'Presenting symptomatology of adopted children', *Archives of General Psychiatry*, vol. 20, no. 1, pp. 110—16.*

145 REEVES, A.C. (1971)

'Children with surrogate parents; cases seen in analytic therapy and an aetiological hypothesis', *British Journal of Medical Psychology*, vol. 44, no. 2, pp. 155—71.
A careful description and discussion of two cases of adoption and one of foster care which had been treated by analytic therapy. The stages of treatment relationship are described and an explanatory hypothesis is formulated for the apthogenesis.

**146 SCHECHTER, M.D.,
TOUSSIENG, P.W. and
GILMARTIN, R.C.
(1967)**

'Adoption problems and the physician', *Current Medical Digest*, vol. XXXIV, no. 6, pp. 821—38.

A commentary on a wide range of adoption literature over about ten years in USA concerned in some way with the relation of adoption to the need for psychiatric and counselling services, and the roles that physicians may find themselves playing as they come in contact with adopted children and adoptive families.

**147 SCHULTZ,
AMELIA L. and
MOTULSKY, ARNO G.
(1971)**

'Medical genetics and adoption', *Child Welfare*, vol. 50, no. 1, pp. 414—17.

This article assembles enough of the terms, definitions and known facts about genetics to be a useful reference for adoption workers. Among the noteworthy points are:

drugs taken by mother during the pregnancy should not be a deterrent to the adoption if a baby is found to be normal by physical examination;

a considerably higher risk of schizophrenia for the relatives of schizophrenics;

epilepsy — incidence in relatives is low;

incest — even in the absence of disease, mental retardation is a significant risk, and observation for some time before placement for adoption is recommended;

genetic diseases are not *ipso facto* untreatable;

genetic counselling is described and recommended.

**148 STANDING
CONFERENCE OF
SOCIETIES
REGISTERED FOR
ADOPTION (1966)**

Medical Aspects of Adoption. 58 pp.

A collection of ten papers read at conferences organized over a period of years. They deal with 'Medical Responsibility in Adoption', the effect of a number of different medical disorders such as neonatal disorders, chest conditions, heart problems and epilepsy. There is an article on adolescence, one on heredity, and a list of references to medical problems in current literature.

**149 STANDING
CONFERENCE OF
SOCIETIES
REGISTERED FOR
ADOPTION (1968)**

Report to the Home Office on difficulties arising from the Adoption Act 1958. 42 pp.

The main headings under which this report is made are:

Problems inherent in the law;

Problems arising from interpretation of the law;

Special requirements and difficulties in certain courts.

Among the major recommendations are:

Consent of natural parents should be required once only and should become legally operative when given;

The role of the guardian *ad litem* should be abolished;

All adoption agencies should be registered with and inspected by the Home Office;

The rights and duties of natural fathers should be reconsidered.

51

150 STANDING
CONFERENCE OF
SOCIETIES
REGISTERED FOR
ADOPTION (1969)

Medical aspects of child adoption. A collection of papers by various authorities. Medical Group Papers I. 100 pp.

This volume contains 10 papers dealing with different aspects of 'The unmarried mother and her child in relation to adoption' delivered at a day conference of the Medical Group of the Standing Conference in 1966, and four papers given at a similar conference in 1967 on 'Some medical and social aspects of adoption'.

151 STEINBERG,
DAYAN MEYER (1969)

Responsum on Problems of Adoption in Jewish Law. Office of the Chief Rabbi, London. 46 pp.

An examination of the problems in Jewish law raised by the adoption of children by Jewish or Anglo-Jewish couples. Only some of these children are registered with the Beth Din. One point of importance is that membership of the Jewish community depends on birth and family, not on legal adoption. Any child brought up in the house of a Jewish couple has rights established by that very fact, but even if legally adopted according to English law, rights of inheritance are not established in Jewish law, and the child retains rights of inheritance from his natural parents. Procedures and registration forms according to Jewish law are given.

152 WALSH, ETHEL D. and LEWIS, FRANCES S. (1969)

'A study of adoptive mothers in a child guidance clinic', *Social Casework*, vol. 50, no. 10, pp. 587—94.

A study of 12 women who had adopted children, and who had come to the attention of a child guidance clinic in Boston, Mass., in a five-year period. The major common source of difficulty seemed to be the guilt they had about taking children who did not belong to them, a guilt that arose from the unresolved anger and rivalry they had felt for their own mothers.

153 WESSEL, MORRIS A. (1966)

'A paediatrician views adoption and unwed adolescent parenthood', *Child Welfare*, vol. 45, no. 6, pp. 334—7.

A discussion by a paediatrician of the role he can play in helping an adoptive couple at crucial points: preparing to receive a baby (pre-placement visit) and adjusting to the new role when the baby has arrived; at nine to ten months with the baby's first independent activity; telling the child of his adoption, preferably when the child is four to five years old.

He can serve a useful function too as the agency consultant in helping to explain to the adopters the physical condition of a newborn child, and to present to the adoptive couple — in the presence of the social worker — the medical diagnosis and the extent of necessary treatment where the child being adopted has some physical defect or limitation.

He recommends a co-ordinated educational, medical and casework programme for teenagers as soon as pregnancy is suspected, so that a well devised plan can be made including continued education at school if the girl wants it.

SECTION IV
Literature on adoption and allied matters

154 BILLINGSLEY, ANDRES and GIOVANNONI, JEANNE (1969)

'Research Perspectives in Interracial Adoption', *Race, Research and Reason*, National Association of Social Workers, New York, 74 pp.

A thorough-going review of interracial adoption — the background, the available figures, the underlying assumptions, and its limitations as a means of dealing with the outstanding needs of children. A list of a dozen reports is given, and some space devoted to three racial types — Oriental, American Indian and negro. Ten general trends in interracial adoption are listed, and some alternatives to interracial adoption are considered — including stimulating adoption by negro families, the use of long-term foster-care, and a form of guardianship.

155 BLUTH, HOWARD (1967)

'Factors in the decision to adopt independently', *Child Welfare*, vol. 46, no. 9, pp. 504—13.

This study showed that the majority of couples who adopted independently would have preferred to adopt through an agency. The most important barrier had been the religious requirements of the agencies.

156 BOWERBANK, M.W. (1970)

'The case-committee — what is its future?', *Child Adoption*, vol. 59, no. 1, pp. 35—8.

An examination of the value and function of adoption case-committees on the basis of the experience of one of them, the Western National Adoption Society, Bath. While making a tentative definition, it appeals for a further study of the subject.

157 CHEVLIN, MYRON R. (1967)

'Adoption outlook', *Child Welfare*, vol. 46, no. 2, pp. 75—82, 106.

A discussion of the development of adoption in the United States, based on the figures for 1962—4, which showed an increase from 62,900 non-relative adoptions to 71,600. Concern is expressed for Federal money to be made available to support agency work, and about the increasing strain on available qualified social workers. Special attention is paid to the Code of Standards for adoption, to inter-racial adoptions, single-parent adoptions and religious questions, and the relative merits of independent and agency adoptions.

158 CHILD ADOPTION (1970)

'Adoption in Surrey', *Child Adoption*, vol. 59, no. 1, pp. 52—6.

The Children's Officer reports on the work of the Adoption Agency during a ten year period, 1959—69 during which time 1,425 babies were placed and 1,261 orders made. An attempt is described to control the balance between the number of approved adopters and the number of children. The experience with follow-up group discussions is described.

159 CHILD ADOPTION (1970)

'A history of child adoption in Northern Ireland', *Child Adoption*, vol. 61, no. 3, pp. 23—6.

This article contains information obtained by the Northern Ireland Child Welfare Council and presented to the Minister of Home Affairs in a report in 1962. In addition to this, information covering the period 1929—62 and some statistics are given for the year ended 31 March 1969.

160 CHILD WELFARE (1970)

'Abortion and Adoption', *Child Welfare*, vol. 49, no. 10, p. 544.

This editorial comment on the effect of more readily available abortion in several American states, warns against confusing the needs of the unmarried mother with the needs of childless couples, and treating one as merely the answer to the other. It is urged that the needs of childless couples be sought by freeing more children in foster care for adoption and by more research into the causes of infertility.

161 CONSUMERS' ASSOCIATION (1969)

How to adopt. 143 pp.

A summary of essential information about the procedure of adoption, how to go about it, and some of the considerations to have in mind.

162 DEASY, LEILA and MULLANEY, JOAN W. (1970)

'The suburban white and the adoption of children', *Social Service Review*, vol. 44, no. 3.*

163 DEMBROSKI, B.G. and JOHNSON, D.L. (1969)

'Dogmatism and attitudes towards adoption', *Marriage and the Family*, vol. 31, no. 4, pp. 788—92.

An examination of attitudes to adoption was carried out with 113 college students (61 men and 52 women) to see if they were related to 'dogmatism' (a closed-mind, rigid attitude in general), and whether there were sex differences. It was found that men who are dogmatic in general are also intolerant in their attitudes towards adoption, but that this was not so for women. Men and women tended to agree in their judgements on specific points however, for example, that intellectual deprivation is more damaging than physical handicap.

164 ERICKSON, M. (1969)

'Adoption facilitating service: a method of strengthening and extending services', *Child Welfare*, vol. 48, no. 10, pp. 620—5.

In face of the rapid increase of adoptions in the United States, (from 93,000 in 1955 to 152,000 in 1966) and the estimated 60,000 children available for adoption but hard to place (because of age, race or handicaps) a campaign has been undertaken in the Midwest Region. An account is given here of some of the findings, and of the work of the Midwest Adoption Facilitating Service and its national equivalent the Adoption Resource Exchange of North America.

165 FELLNER, I.W. (1968)

'Recruiting adoptive applicants', *Social Work*, vol. 13, no. 1, pp. 92—100.

An examination is made of the large number of 'minority group' children, and of older children, available for adoption in the United States but not adopted because of lack of applicants. The methods of agencies are critically reviewed, and the use of adoption exchanges favourably noted.

166 GROW, LUCILLE J. and SMITH, MICHAEL J. (1971)

'Adoption Trends: 1969—70', *Child Welfare*, vol. 50, no. 7, pp. 401—7.

A comparison of selected data from some public and voluntary agencies, shows some falling off (18 per cent) in the number of children accepted for adoption, some increase (4 per cent) in the number of applications to adopt, and some increase (6 per cent) in the percentage of homes approved per 100 children needing them. The variations as between white and non-white children and adopters and between the experience of public and voluntary agencies is shown.

167 HELLER, ELSIE (1966)

'Applications by married parents for adoptive placement of their in-wedlock children', *Child Welfare*, vol. 45, no. 7, pp. 404—9.

This paper presents the facts and discusses the implications of applications by married couples for their unborn baby to be adopted. The numbers throughout the country appear to be around 13,000 a year (20 per cent of all non-relative adoptions) but the Westchester Adoption Service, New York, from which this paper comes have a very much smaller proportion, and the paper is based on the fifteen couples who actually released their in-wedlock child for adoption. The concern is about the best ways to serve these applicants to come to the right decision, and some typical examples are quoted.

168 HUMPHREY, MICHAEL (1966)

'Childless marriage as a basis for adoption', *Mental Health*, vol. 25, no. 4, pp. 17—18.

A discussion of ways in which the motivation and suitability of childless couples may be inferred in the process of considering them as prospective adopters.

169 INFAUSTO, F.
(1969)

'Perspectives on adoption', *Annals*, vol. 383, N. Y. State Department of Social Services, pp. 1—12.*

170 JEHU, DEREK
(1968)

'Developmental issues in interracial adoptions', *Case Conference*, vol. 14, no. 9, pp. 345—9.

A review of some of the literature on the effect of heredity and environmental factors on such things as intelligence, skin colour and certain forms of behaviour. The importance of the environmental conditions in producing variations in individual performance and behaviour is urged as an encouragement to adoptive parents who might otherwise be unduly apprehensive about the effect of 'bad stock'.

171 KADUSHIN,
ALFRED (1970)

'Adoptive status: birth parents *v.* bread parents', *Child Care Quarterly Review*, vol. 24, no. 1, pp. 10—14.

A discussion of the attitude of adoptive parents to adoption — the difference between accepting their adoptive status, and themselves as 'bread parents'; and thinking of their family as an 'ordinary' family and themselves as 'birth parents'. The discussion is based on interviews with ninety-one couples, and quotations from the tape-recordings made of the interviews.

172 KADUSHIN,
ALFRED (1970)

'Single-Parent adoptions: an over-view and some relevant research', *The Social Service Review*, vol. 44, no. 3, pp. 263—74.

This article reviews the problems and advantages of single-parent adoptions. It details the limited agency experience in the United States with such adoptions, the agency eligibility requirements in such adoptions, and the rationale for such requirements. It is noted that a principal determinant to agency acceptance of such a procedure is the supposition that single parenthood is necessarily pathological. A review of relevant research is presented suggesting that the single-parent family is merely a variant child-rearing context and not inherently or necessarily pathogenic.

173 KELLMER
PRINGLE, M.L. (1967)

Adoption — facts and fallacies. Longmans, in association with National Children's Bureau, 252 pp.

A comprehensive review of research projects, and reports on them, from the United States, Canada and Great Britain between 1948 and 1965. The abstracts of completed research projects are classified according to their material, and the annotated bibliography is arranged according to categories of subject matter. The sources of information, and where to obtain access to full reports, are given, and a composite bibliography makes reference easy.

In the chapters of write-up the scheme is outlined, the material reviewed as a whole, and the 'facts, figures, and fallacies' are summarized and the routes along which adoption practice seems to be moving are briefly traced — freedom of communication between the parties to adoption; a social work service for both natural parents and adoptive families before and after the adoption and the placement of a child.

174 KERMACK, STUART O. (1968)

'Thoughts on adoption procedures', *Child Adoption*, vol. 54, pp. 39—41.

Describes the unsatisfactory state of affairs from the point of view of the Scottish court and the Sheriff. He recommends abolishing the curator *ad litem* and giving greater responsibility to the placement and supervizing agencies. He questions whether the Sheriff's court is the right tribunal to handle adoptions. He questions the present use being made of adoption to cover up illegitimacy and create a legal lie.

175 KHATRI, A.A. and SIDDIQUI, B.B. (1969)

'A boy or a girl?: preferences of parents for sex of offspring as perceived by East Indian and American children: a cross-cultural study', *Journal of Marriage and the Family*, vol. 31, no. 2, pp. 388—92.

Entirely concerned with the mother's and father's preferences for boys and girls as seen by children at the age of 8 and the age of 11. The method was to tell an adoption story and get the children's responses. Comparison is made between the results obtained from 148 Indian children and 119 American children.

176 KITTSON, RUTHENA H. (1968)

Orphan Voyage. Vantage Press. 259 pp.

The writer was herself adopted. She recounts here, largely in narrative form, how she came to establish in Philadelphia the Life History Study Center, now called Orphan Voyage, to enable grown up people who have been adopted to get in touch with their natural parents. In the process the feelings and experiences of these and other relatives, and of a certain number of adoptive parents, have been gathered together in the form of letters, and accounts of interviews.

177 KNIGHT, IRIS G. (1970)

'The handicapped child', *Child Adoption*, vol. 61, no. 3, pp. 33—8.

A discussion of handicaps of various sorts and varying severity, with their accompanying emotional states, and their effect on family life.

178 KNIGHT, IRIS G. (1970)

'Placing the handicapped child for adoption', *Child Adoption*, vol. 62, no. 4, pp. 27—35.

A discussion of the placement of handicapped children for adoption. Among the important points made are:
handicapped children must be placed early;
homes can be found for the majority of babies previously thought unsuitable on grounds of hereditary risk, e.g. children with epileptic, diabetic or allergic disorder in their background;

hereditary risk of mental disorder presents more difficulty;
for handicapped children, atypical applicants may be considered, e.g. those who have had children, those older than are normally accepted, those who themselves have minor medical problems, etc.;
importance of the adoption officer and the medical officer having real experience of handicapped children;
vital importance of general practitioner of adopting family being involved and favourable beforehand;
necessity of local community offering facilities required by child's handicap.

179 KNIGHT, IRIS G.
(1971)

'Placement of children into families with a seriously handicapped child', *Child Adoption*, vol. 63, no. 1, pp. 56—9.
A discussion of whether the presence of a seriously handicapped child in a family makes the adoption of a child out of the question. After consideration of several actual applications — where the child of the family suffered from haemophilia, congenital heart disease, minor cerebral palsy, or was a mongol — concluded that adoption would be unwise.

180 KNIGHT, IRIS G.
(1971)

'Applicants with severe handicaps', *Child Adoption*, vol. 64, no. 2, pp. 35—9.
Consideration of the possibilities and problems of placing a child for adoption with parents, one of whom suffers from a serious handicap — defective sight or hearing, a cleft palate, diabetes, people dependent on a kidney machine etc. — leads to the conclusion that though not absolutely barred, the demands on the adopters are exceptional, and placements will be rare.

181 KORNITZER,
MARGARET (1968)

Adoption and Family Life. Putnam, London, 252 pp.
This study of adoptions, and the families in which they have taken place, extended over 13 years, and covered 503 adoption situations involving 664 children (at all stages of their lives). The sources included two national societies and two county authorities. Results are presented where possible in statistical form, but the most valuable 'evidence' is the long-term impressions of the writer, who is careful to put her findings in this form rather than as conclusions. Among these, however, are the following: the far-reaching danger of 'secrecy' and its deleterious effects on adopters and adopted and their mutual relationships; the 'infected' attitude common among all parties — children, adopting family and members of the public — of expecting trouble and 'waiting for it to appear'; the value of continuing the possibility of 'third party' adoptions; the advantage of placing children over twelve months with a younger rather than with an older adopting mother; and the positive values of the adoptive situation which have not yet been fully explored.

182 KORNITZER,
MARGARET (1971)

'The adopted adolescent and the sense of identity',
Child Adoption, vol. 66, no. 4, pp. 43—8.

A draft of some 'Notes for adoptive parents' dealing with the needs of adopted children, particularly at adolescence, for help in developing their sense of identity when they are without knowledge of their natural parents. 'What is the nature of the need?' and 'How can it be helped?' are the questions which are considered.

183 KRUGMAN,
DOROTHY C. (1967)

'Differences in the relation of parents and children to adoption', *Child Welfare*, vol. 46, no. 5, pp. 267—71.

The difference in the attitudes of parents and children to adoption is discussed. The parents have to cope with their own feelings about infertility and parenting someone else's child. The child has to cope with questions of identity when they arise, usually after the age of two. The aim of the article is to help professional workers to support both parents and children in dealing with the questions that are really bothering them, and not protect them from situations that are not real in their lives.

184 LAUNAY, Cl.
(1966)

'Le couple adoptant', *Revue de hygiene et medicine sociale*, vol. 14, no. 5, pp. 469—79.

An informed discussion of the adoption process from the point of view of the adopters, beforehand, at the time, and in cases of disappointment through absence of available children. Most attention is given to telling the child about his adoption, and the haunting spectre of heredity. Cases of psychiatric breakdown are thought to be rare, but serious.

185 LAUNAY, Cl.
(1968)

'Problemes actuels poses par l'adoption', *Presse medicale*, vol. 76, no. 39, pp. 1879—80.

A discussion of incidence of personality difficulties among adopted children, based on the frequency of referrals to psychiatric clinics; and the effects of the new adoption law of July 1966, in France.

186 LUSK, J.T. (1968)

'Co-operation between doctors and social workers in adoption', *Child Adoption*, vol. 53, pp. 33—42.

A description of some of the points in the adoption process at which doctors and social workers are inevitably in touch, and the ways in which this cooperation has been fostered in the experience of one Scottish agency.

187 LUSK, J.T. (1969)

'Adoption in Scotland', *Child Adoption*, vol. 58, pp. 39—41.

This article is mainly about boarding out, but it is noted that the numbers of foster children who have been adopted has tended to increase but has remained small. Many of the adoptions were however 'a quasi-adoption with no active involvement in rehabilitation'.

Adoption in Brief

188 LUSK, J.T. (1969)

'Adoption in Scotland', *Child Adoption*, vol. 58, no. 3, pp. 11—16.
In this account of adoption in Scotland, under the separate provisions of the Adoption Act 1958, the differences are noted — the curator *ad litem*, and the Scottish court system, the scarcity of moral welfare workers, and the consequent uneven and inadequate provision of services for unmarried parents. Some account is given of the work of the voluntary societies and the local authorities; the effect of the Social Work (Scotland) Act is speculated on, and the needs of coloured children and handicapped children for adoption.

189 McILVENNA, B.M. (1967)

'Difficult-to-place children', *Child Care News*, no. 67, pp. 2—5.
A report is given of a study of children in care to the Catholic Crusade of Rescue who were hard to place because they had either some non-white admixture in their parentage, or had some physical handicap or a history of disturbed behaviour. Of the different ways of providing for these children, adoption was used in just over a quarter of the cases (57 out of 217). The facts are given; conclusions are not drawn.

190 McWHINNIE, ALEXINA M. (1966)

Adoption assessments. Standing conference of Societies Registered for Adoption, 30 pp.
The pamphlet contains two papers read by Dr. McWhinnie at different times and published in *Child Adoption*, vols. 44 and 46, dealing respectively with (1) a team approach used by the Guild of Service in Edinburgh in assessing both children offered for adoption and adoptive applicants, and (2) further notes about 'Adoption Placements', including the use of groups methods with adoptive parents.

191 McWHINNIE, ALEXINA M. (1970)

'Who am I?', *Child Adoption*, vol. 62, pp. 36—40.
A strong plea for freedom for adopted children to be able to consult adoption records after a certain age, as in Scotland, so as to satisfy proper curiosity about their personal identity. The evidence of the follow-up study of adults who had been adopted is used (see McWhinnie, 'Adopted Children; how they grow up' 1967).

192 MADISON, BERNICE (1966)

'Adoption: yesterday, to-day and tomorrow', 2 parts, *Child Welfare*, vol. 45, no. 5, pp. 253—8 and vol. 45, no. 6, pp. 341—8.
Part I describes the changing attitudes to adoption in the American States, the strengthening of adoption laws, the growing interest in adopting children and the expansion of the services. There is a review of current agency practices, and a survey of some of the research.
In Part II an attempt is made to forecast the developments likely to take place in the future, and it is concluded among other things that only a minority of the children will be adopted who would, on

60

the face of it, benefit from being adopted. Thirty per cent of illegitimate children are adopted. There is little reliable information about the 70 per cent who remain with their mothers or are looked after by relatives or in foster homes.

193 MILLS, ROSEMARY (1966)

'Disabled adopted girls', *Child Care*, vol. 20, no. 2, pp. 46—52.

Details are given of seven Chinese girls in Singapore who after adoption developed a permanent disabling condition, and their subsequent history. The attitude of the adopting parents to the disablement was related to their motive for adopting, e.g. to fulfil a need of the adoptive parents, or because the mother wanted to care for and bring up children.

194 MITCHELL, MARION M. (1969)

'Transracial adoptions: philosophy and practice', *Child Welfare*, vol. 48, no. 10, pp. 613—19.

A summary of impressions arising from the placement of some hundreds of non-white children with 'caucasian' parents in various parts of U.S.A. and Canada, and some specific local studies of the results. Among other things it was found that infertility was not important, and that the adopting parents were above average in education, income and occupation.

195 MOONEY, MARGARET (1971)

'Adoption anxieties', *Midwife and Health Visitor*, vol. 7, no. 2, pp. 65—7.

A discussion of the ways in which a health visitor can help to smooth the way for a successful adoption in the course of her visits when a baby is placed with a couple and some of the anxieties most commonly met with.

196 MOORE, JOYCE (1968)

'Adoption in Denmark', *Child Adoption*, vol. 54, pp. 31—7.

A description of the adoption work done by the Mothers' Aid Societies in Denmark, with particular reference to the Copenhagen Mothers' Aid, including the service to adoption applicants, unmarried or unsupported mothers, and putative fathers, and the availability of abortion.

197 NOTTINGHAM-SHIRE COUNTY COUNCIL CHILDREN'S DEPARTMENT (1968)

Ninth follow-up of children previously assessed as suitable for adoption 1960—6. 3 pp. Duplicated.

A summary of brief particulars ascertained in a follow-up after six years of 36 children placed for adoption. Some facts about the natural parents, and assessments of the children's intelligence are given.

198 OGER, JEAN (1971)

Des parents comme les autres. ALFA Quai Mativa 68, 4000 Liege. 164 pp.

A popular presentation of a number of real life examples showing from different points of view (e.g. the adoptive mother, the father, the children and the outsider) what is the role of adoptive parents, and supporting the contention that their relationship with their adopted children is as real, even if different, as if the link were biological.

199 OLDS, C.B. (1970)

'Early legal adoption', *Child Welfare*, vol. 49, no. 7, pp. 392—4.

An experiment from 1961—8 in allowing adoptive parents to take their adoption application to court at any time after the placement when they felt ready, but continuing to provide a supportive casework service if desired. As there is no state law insisting on a minimum waiting period, an increasing number of adoptions have been granted under six months, and under three months from placement, the practice is recommended.

200 ORLOVA, NINA V. (1970)

'Adoption in the USSR', *Child Adoption*, vol. 60, no. 2, pp. 35—6.

Reference is made to notes by Professor Orlova which appeared in *International Child Welfare* for October 1969. Adoption had been banned in 1918 but was reintroduced in 1926. Adoption of children up to eighteen years of age is allowed, and is the responsibility of the Ministry of Health for children under four, and of the Ministry of Education for those who are older. The consent of parents is not necessary if they have been deprived of parental rights, or if they have not maintained any link for at least a year with their child in a residential home. Race, religion, and nationality play no part in adoption. It is not at present extensively practised, but figures are not available.

201 O'ROURKE, HELEN (1968)

'The agency as seen through the eyes of its clients', *Child Welfare*, vol. 47, no. 8, pp. 470—7.

This is the report of a survey made by the staff of the Alice Hunt Centre, Cleveland, Ohio, of the views of 75 unwed mothers who had used the agency. They recorded their reactions to the agency and its staff at the start of casework treatment, and again at the termination of service. Their expectations were compared with what they actually found.

202 OUNSTED, CHRISTOPHER (1970)

'The dark side of adoption', *Child Adoption*, vol. 63, no. 1, pp. 23—36.

An examination of some individual adoptive cases referred for psychiatric treatment, leading to the following conclusions, among others:
early placement and good matching are the keystones of adoption;
the 'blood tie' has no scientific basis;
possession and responsibility should be linked legally, to avoid children being treated as chattels.

203 PETTIGREW, BRENDA (1969)

'Group discussion with adoptive parents', *Child Adoption*, vol. 56, no. 1, pp. 39—42.

A description of a series of group meetings for intending adoptive couples, mentioning the topics that arose, and the ancillary purposes that the discussions seemed to serve.

204 PETTIGREW, BRENDA (1970)

'A group of optimists', *Child Adoption*, vol. 59, no. 1, pp. 42—4.

A description of a short series of discussions with prospective adopters arranged for the Agnostics Adoptior Society (now the Independent Adoption Society), the subjects that were broached, the attitudes thet revealed themselves, and some evaluation of the series for those involved.

205 PRO JUVENTUTE (1968)

Pro juventute, vol. 49, no. 4/5. Whole number devoted to adoption.*

206 RAYNOR, LOIS (1967)

'The British adoption project; report of a talk given to the maternity group of medical social workers on 16th November 1966', *Medical Social Work*, vol. 19. no. 9, pp. 305—6.

See Raynor (1971), *Adoption of non-white children*, where the topic is dealt with more fully.

207 RAYNOR, LOIS (1971)

Adoption of non-white children. Allen & Unwin, 210 pp.

An account of the British Adoption Project mounted by the International Social Service of Great Britain in association with the Sociology Department of Bedford College, London, to arrange a number of adoptions of non-white children and study their outcome. One result was the formation of the Adoption Resource Exchange, to bring together applicants and available children, even though they live in different parts of the country. The study showed that there is a considerable residue of non-white children available for adoption who are not adopted; one hindrance being the reluctance of agencies to devote more time to it, or their lack of social workers for the purpose. Groups were used before placement and after the order had been made, and were considered valuable.

208 RICHARDS, KIRSTINE (1970)

'When biological mothers meet adopters', *Child Adoption*, vol. 60, no. 2, pp. 27—30.

The experience of one child care officer, who found that only a small proportion (about 2 per cent) of mothers want to meet prospective adopters, but they want to very badly. A particular instance is described, by way of illustration.

209 RIDAY, EDWIN (1969)

'Supply and demand in adoption', *Child Welfare*, vol. 48, no. 8, pp. 489—91.

An examination of the differences in adoption statistics in 1967 compared with 1958, showing the differences between the public and voluntary agencies, and the growing gap between the placement chances for white and non-white children available for adoption.

210 ROHR, FRANZ
(1971)

'How parents tell their children they are adopted', *Child Welfare*, vol. 50, no. 5, pp. 298—300.

An extract from a booklet of the Children's Home Society of California, which discusses how adoptive parents should talk to their adopted children about the biological parents. It suggests 'first mother' and 'first father' as suitable words to use. The child needs to achieve a sense of identity and be able to 'accept' his first parents, without feelings of rejection and guilt. There is also the difficult matter of coming to terms with illegitimacy, and the danger of the reflection in the child of residual anxieties in his adoptive parents.

211 ROWE, JANE
(1966)

Parents, children and adoption workers. Routledge & Kegan Paul, 294 pp.

A comprehensive treatment of the whole theme of adoption. Part One: 'The Natural Parents', includes a separate chapter on 'The Unmarried Father'; Part Two: 'Heredity and Environment'; Part Three: 'The Creation of New Families' deals with the whole procedure of home-finding, and the actual placement; and Part Four gives the 'Statutory and Legal Requirements'.

A clearing house or adoption exchange on the American pattern is recommended for promoting the adoption of 'hard-to-place' children. Group meetings for adoption applicants are recommended. The problems associated with the function of Adoption Committees are discussed, and some follow-up help to rejected couples is advocated. The value of post-adoption help for the adopters and for adopted teenagers is also discussed.

212 ROWE, JANE
(1969)

'Aspects of adoption — 1 & 2', *Mother and Child*, vol. 41, no. 1, pp. 20—4, no. 2, pp. 20—3.

Two articles made up of extracts from *Yours by Choice* (see Rowe 1969) covering most aspects of adoption for the general reader.

213 ROWE, JANE
(1969, revised edition)

Yours by choice. Routledge & Kegan Paul, 148 pp.

This is a revised edition of the book first published in 1959, which is a practical guide for prospective adoptive parents and covers all most people want to know: reasons for wanting to adopt, the type of children available, alternatives to adoption, questions of heredity and environment, legal requirements, how to obtain the child, preparing for it, telling it about adoption, and special problems of adolescence.

214 ROWE, JANE
(1970)

'The realities of adoptive parenthood', *Child Adoption*, vol. 59, pp. 23—9.

A discussion of the question 'Who is the adopted child's "real" mother?' — the one who gave birth, or the one who provided parenting? The literature is briefly referred to and the dilemma explored. One conclusion is: '. . . adoptive parents need education for their special tasks. Their role is not laid down by tradition and learned automatically in the course of growing up. There is a genuine problem in being the "real" parent and yet at the same time accepting the birth parent'.

215 ROWE, JANE (1971)

'The reality of the adoptive family' in Tod, Robert, Ed. *Social Work in Adoption* [q.v. (231)]. Longman, Chapter 14.

216 RUTTER, MICHAEL (1970)

'Psychological development — predictions from infancy', *Journal of Child Psychology and Psychiatry*, vol. 11, no. 1, pp. 49—62.

A paper on prediction from infancy of later psychological development with particular reference to (a) the diagnosis of pathology, and (b) 'matching' babies with the characteristics or wishes of adoptive parents. It is concluded that at the age of 6 months some estimate may be made of the existence of psychological pathology, but no useful predictions can be made of psychological characteristics within the normal range. (This paper is included in 'Medical Group Papers II', see p. 76 Association of British Adoption Agencies 1970).

217 SARMIENTO, I.M. (1969)

'Adoption week: a publicity project in adoptive recruitment', *Child Welfare*, vol. 48, no. 3, pp. 166—9.

Initiated in 1963 by Los Angeles County Department of Adoptions, and continued by BABY (Bureau Auxiliary Board for Youngsters) particularly concerned with the needs of the Negro and Mexican communities, and there has been a steady increase of placements of non-white children (Negro children placed: 1957 — 506; 1966 — 2,503).

218 SCHOENBERG, C. (1970)

'Abortion and Adoption', *Child Welfare*, vol. 49, no. 10, p. 5440.

An editorial comment on the issues involved in abortion legislation, and its effect on adoption practice, together with a reference to the treatment of infertility.

219 SELDEN, JEAN and GUMBINER, JOSEPHINE S. (1969)

'A parents' adoption league', *Child Welfare*, vol. 43, no. 3, p. 165.

Describes the setting up of a Parents' Adoption League by the Los Angeles County Department of Adoptions in 1964 for people who had adopted children from the agency. The activities and values are briefly summarized.

220 SELLERS, MARTHA G. (1969)

'Trans-racial adoption', *Child Welfare*, vol. 48, no. 5, pp. 355—6.

In a study of white applicants for black or mixed racial children for adoption in Chicago, fourteen criteria were distinguished which bore on their suitability, of which the most important were compatible motivation, education and awareness and ability to allow the child to accept his racial identity.

221 SENSEL, BARBARA and YEAKEL, MARGARET (1970)

'Relationship capacity and "acknowledgement of difference" in adoptive parenthood', *Smith College studies in social work*, vol. 40, no. 2, pp. 155—63.

Results show a significant relation between capacity for mature object relationships and 'acknowledgement of difference' of the adoptive situation. Parents' capacities to relate well in a variety of situations may be a crucial index of the ability to take on adoptive parenthood.

222 SHARRAR, MARY LOU (1970)

'Some helpful techniques when placing older children for adoption', *Child Welfare*, vol. 48, no. 8, pp. 459—63.

Describes techniques recommended by the writer for adoptive parents of children over six months when adopted. For the non-verbal child of six to 18 months she suggests songs about adoption, and for the verbal, over 18 months, she provides stories rehearsing the adoption situation for the parents to read or tell. Examples are given.

223 SHARRAR, MARY LOU (1971)

'Attitude of black natural parents regarding adoption', *Child Welfare*, vol. 50, no. 5, pp. 286—9.

Group methods reduced the antagonism, and increased the understanding of the girls, particularly as a result of meeting adoptive parents.

224 SHIREMAN, JOAN F. (1970)

'Adoptive applicants who withdraw', *Social Service Review*, vol. 44, no. 3, pp. 285—92.*

225 SOULE, M. and NOELE, J. (1970)

'Les problemes psychologiques de la sterilite et ceux de l'adoption', *Gazette medicale de France*, vol. 77, no. 29, pp. 6057—66.

A description of the inner feelings of couples who have to come to terms with their own incapacity to produce a child, and with the fact that a child placed with them for adoption is not their own — attitudes to the natural mother, and fears about a tainted heredity.

226 SPENCER, JOHN C. (1969)

'Putative and fugitive fathers', *Child Adoption*, vol. 57, no. 2, pp. 39—43.

A paper read to the Scottish Council for the Unmarried Mother and Her Child summarizing what little is known with certainty about putative fathers, and what emerges from the limited (American) literature about working with putative fathers. Some conclusions are drawn affecting court procedures and social policy.

227 STANDING CONFERENCE OF SOCIETIES REGISTERED FOR ADOPTION (1968)

Adoption Involving Mixed Races. 27 pp.

Four papers read at a day conference in June 1967 dealing with developmental issues in interracial adoption, the special demands made by interracial adoption, and the cultural patterns in family life in the West Indies, and in India and Pakistan.

223 STANDING CONFERENCE OF SOCIETIES REGISTERED FOR ADOPTION (1968)

Report on area of residence survey. Association of British Adoption Agencies, 12 pp.

A brief examination of movements of mothers and babies involved in 4,448 adoption placements in England and Wales and 316 in Scotland. This showed the expected movement of mothers from counties and small boroughs to large urban centres during their pregnancy and the birth of the baby, and a movement out again for temporary foster care and adoption placement.

229 STONE, F.H. (1969)

'Adoption and identity', *Child Adoption*, vol. 58, no. 3, pp. 17—28.

An exposition by a psychiatrist of the nature of 'identity' and 'identification' and what it means in the adoption situation. Examples are given of couples interviewed with a view to adoption, and of adopted children referred for behaviour difficulties. Implications are drawn about 'matching', 'telling', and the sense of loss.

230 THOMAS, MORLAIS (1971)

'A contribution (on the work of voluntary societies in adoption)', *Social Service News*, vol. 1, no. 8, pp. 6—8.

The figures for the placement of 'hard-to-place' children by the Church of England Children's Society in 1967, 1968, 1969 and 1970 in 'Boarding out with a view to adoption' are examined. The numbers were between 160 and 200 per year and the breakdown rate varied from 4 per cent to 1 per cent. The number of children with one or both parents of non-European origin is shown, and there is a breakdown of the age of the children at placement. It is concluded that much more might be done in this sphere if agencies are prepared to devote adequate resources of time, money and man-power to it.

231 TOD, ROBERT J.N., Ed. (1971)

Social work in adoption: collected papers. Longman. (Longman papers on social work), 158 pp.

Fourteen papers, from four British and ten American sources, covering various aspects of adoption, including: underlying principles and assumptions, the unmarried mother, the unmarried father, the adoption of the older child, supervision, group methods (three papers), and a final chapter, written especially for this volume by Jane Rowe on 'The reality of the adoptive family'.

232 TOMBS, DAVID (1966)

'Adoption in Ontario', *Child Care News*, no. 52, pp. 9—13.

A description of adoption in the State of Ontario, under the Child Welfare Act, 1965. Out of 6,245 adoptions completed in a twelve month period, 4,730 were agency placements. No guardian *ad litem* is appointed. The influence of the mass media and of the ten-year-old Adoption Resource Exchange are discussed.

233 TOUSSIENG, P.W. (1971)

'Realising the potential in adoptions', *Child Welfare*, vol. 50, no. 6, pp. 322—7.

The writer comes to the conclusion that better results would be obtained if adopters did not try to pretend that the adopted child was their 'biologic' child, and if the adoption agencies revised their philosophy and got away from the pretence that they are placing a perfect, and perfectly matched child, who will be indistinguishable from a 'biologic' child. Moreover a programme of increased support to the adoptive families after the placement of a child should be developed.

234 WERK, M.B. van de (1966)

'Adoption' (an introductory and informative talk) The Hague, *National Federation for Child Welfare*, 14 pp., duplicated.

A general discussion of the issues present in adoption in the context of Dutch law.

235 YOUNG, JOYCE (1971)

'Adoption in Kenya', *Child Adoption*, vol. 64, no. 2, pp. 19—27.

A report of a visit to Kenya to assess the present position and the needs. Some account of the work of the three existing adoption societies is given, and an indication of the way development should take, particularly in view of the growing industrialization of the urban areas.

236 LAWDER, ELIZABETH A. *et al.* (1971)

'Unwed mothers and their decisions to keep or surrender children', *Child Welfare*, vol. 50, no. 4, pp. 253—61.

Variables consistently associated in this study and others with mothers' decisions to keep their children were: older age, employment status (not in school) and non-intact parental home. Some others add lower education. The decision to keep a child may be the result of a host of emotional needs and conflicts. The consistent finding that women who stem from broken homes are more likely to keep their children may be related.

Author Index